Fearlessly Yours,
Mary Ann
Halpin

FEARLESS WOMEN

FEARLESS WISDOM

PHOTOGRAPHY BY MARY ANN HALPIN

FOREWORD BY SANDRA YANCEY

STORY EDITORS
DR. JOYCE MILLS AND GAIL SPECKMANN

FEARLESS WOMEN PUBLISHING, LOS ANGELES

FOREWORD

It is with great honor and pride that I encourage you to read a book which captures both the beauty and brilliance of some amazingly powerful women who are committed to living their dreams and monetizing their passions. I know their stories will make a difference in your life as you capture their glow and embrace your own!

I remember my own "fearless woman" experience a few years back. I received the inaugural Fearless Women book as a gift from my dear girlfriend, Marilyn Tam, who was one of the dynamic women featured in the book. I slowly perused the photos and the stories. I was drawn to the sword—such a symbol of fierce conviction. I knew I needed my own experience—to hold that blade in my hands and garner the strength from the women who had held it before me, women such as Cybill Shepherd, Joni Mitchell, and Shari Belafonte. So, I made my appointment and traveled to Hollywood to have my photo session. Never one to boast comfortably, this photo session was as much about honoring my internal strength and beauty as it was honoring my external strength and beauty. I spared no expense—new outfit, freshly cut hair, and make-up artist. It was, after all, a once-in-a-lifetime experience.

With all the details tended to, I walked from the dressing room onto the studio floor. The sword was gently put in my hands. I immediately felt my body engulfed with feminine vigor and potency I had never felt before. My eyes welled with tears, representing the challenges and barriers as well as triumphs and breakthroughs of the women who had held this sword. A softness overcame me. As I looked down, my tears fell to the floor like a light drip of water. Make no mistake about it, however; there is still much strength and power in those tears. I am often reminded that over time and with gentle persistence, a drop of water is capable of eroding a boulder!

The camera started clicking. I posed and posed, wondering what to do with this heavy blade in my hand. Suddenly, I got out of my head and into my heart. The photographer, Mary Ann Halpin, asked me, "Sandra, what do you want the women who see this picture to glean from you?" And there it was, my "truth." I lay the sword across my palms, extended it forward, and said to myself, "Here, take it. I share with you my power, my pain, my strength, my fear, my fearlessness and my wisdom. Pass it on."

And so it is. This book is a culmination of other great women who have taken the sword and now pass it on to you. The title of this book, Fearless Women, Fearless Wisdom, is provocative indeed! I have pondered this word "fearless" for years. In the dictionary, fearless is referenced as synonymous with "courageous—resolute in the face of dangers or challenges." Somehow, this fits better for me. In all honesty, I do experience fear from time to time. I've learned that being a business owner is definitely not about living life in the safe zone. It's also not about sorting everything out to the point where decisions are risk-free.

It is more like, as my mother used to so poignantly say, "Walking to the edge and jumping—and building your wings on the way down." Before I have jumped—or made a decision to take a risk—I have felt fear. In fact, if you are like me, we can let the fear fester for awhile, and in some cases, far too long. Fearless, I think, is a consequence of feeling fear, embracing it with a big hug, finding comfort in the discomfort of it, and doing what causes us fear anyway. If you think about it, the feeling of fearlessness is often a fleeting one, coming and going the instant you make a decision to "go for it." That instant, however, cannot be taken for granted. Like a gentle kiss, the sweet sensation can be life-changing and everlasting. In the end, it takes courage to embrace our fears and become fearless. Courage is the lingering effect which carries us forward.

I believe we must be careful not to smother fear with our fearlessness, as fear certainly has its purpose in life. Perhaps its purpose is that important characteristic we call wisdom. Wisdom allows us to honor fear when it presents itself again, and it undoubtedly will. It reminds us of the power we really have—and it is the power to overcome! Wisdom allows us to smile when fear pops up again. Our smile reflects our familiarity with fear and our wisdom is a comforting reminder that "we know better"— that we will endure, learn, grow and survive—and will be all the better for it!

Girlfriends, of course, help us along the way. They are our examples of grace and courage, beauty and brilliance, fear and fearlessness, all attributes we strive to emulate. I am privileged to share this book with the 40 extraordinary women who are featured, a common bond that now makes us girlfriends. I applaud them for their courage—their fearlessness to risk sharing their private journeys—and their wisdom to know the difference they will make in the lives of countless others as a result of doing so! I give accolades to Mary Ann Halpin, a dear girlfriend and quintessential "visionary" photographer, for capturing each woman's truth, an art shared by precious few. Through our fears, courage, wisdom and fearlessness, I know my life and journey are better because you, my friend, are in it.

To all the women of the world, may this book represent your personal "knighting" of the sword by honoring what it means to be you, a woman, in today's world. Perhaps this book will take us to the original ceremony of the sword. A bit of HIStory for you—in the beginning, knighthood was conferred by a warm embrace, not just a simple tap on the shoulder. So now, in the spirit of HERstory, I return us to the beginning of time and honor you by extending a big, warm embrace in celebration of your fearlessness and your wisdom!

To your continued success and fearless journey ~
Sandra Yancey
Founder and CEO
eWomenNetwork, Inc.

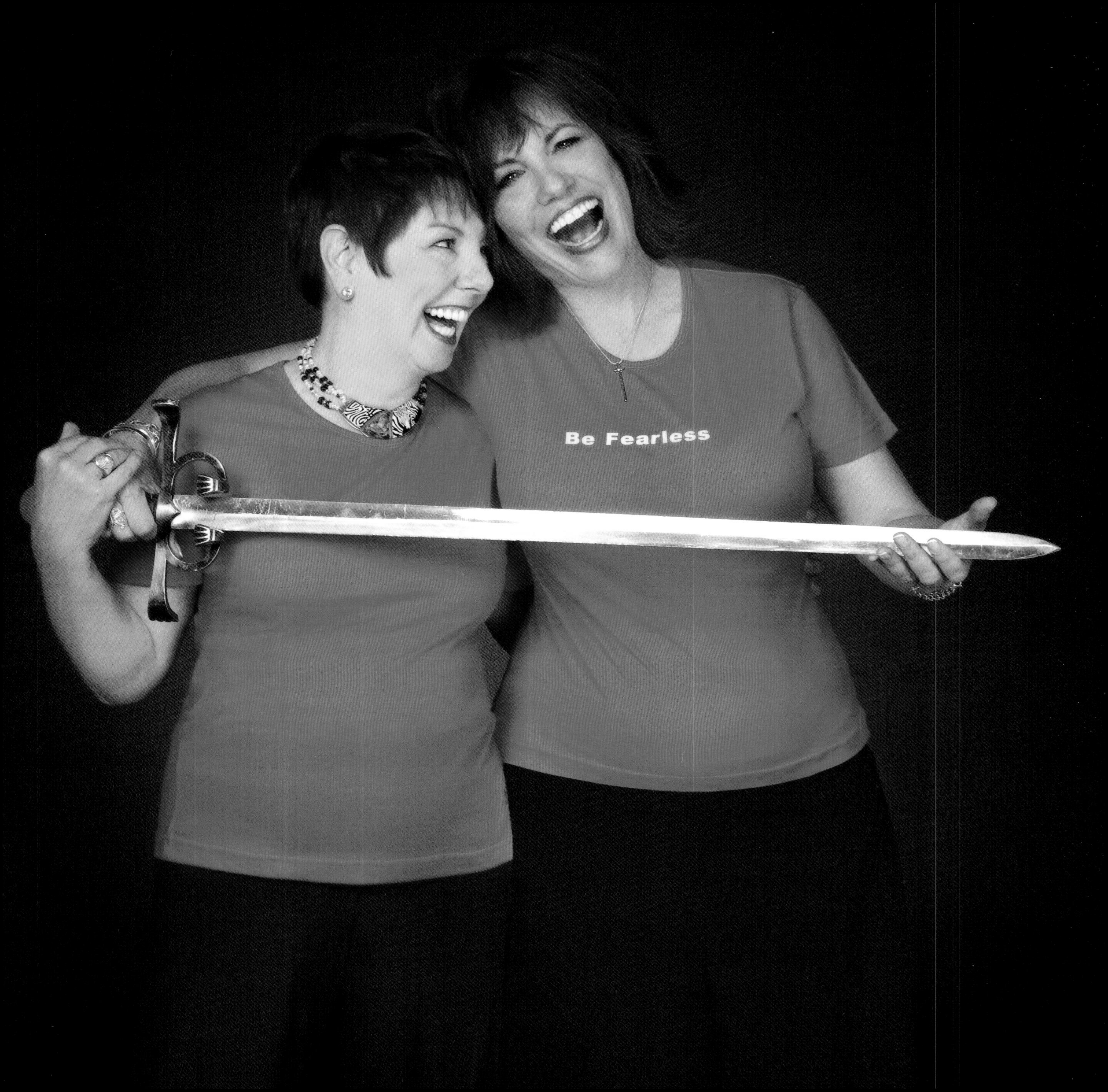
Be Fearless

C O N T E N T S

Foreword

Acknowledgments

Introduction

Anne Marie Hansen   12

Aremita Watson   14

Marina Collazo   16

Wendy Bialek   18

Toni Sexton   20

Deb Greene   22

Marquetta Glass   25

Jean Carpenter-Backus   26

Patti DeNucci   28

Debbie Hoover   30

Peggy Kinst   33

Linda Lee Kaye   34

Sami Douglass   36

Vicki Lynn Klasell   39

Betty Liedtke   41

Juliann Kelley   42

Louise Griffith   44

Lar Park Lincoln   46

Debra Dion Krischke   49

Gloria Manchester   50

Patti Lustig   52

Pamela Bush-Davis   54

Rosemary McDowell   56

Adrienne McGill   58

Joyce C. Mills, Ph.D.   60

Lori Palm   63

Michelle Peavy   65

Mary Pike   66

Paoola Sefair   68

Sandy Shepard   70

Gail Speckmann   73

Patti Waterbury   74

Jacqueline Wales   76

Jenny Telwar   78

Karna Sundby   80

Karie Wood   82

Terri Starnes-Bryant   85

Susan K. Younger   86

Sherí Taber   88

Ruth Thoes Vivrett   90

To My Wise and Fearless Friend   92

Contact   94

Foundation   96

Published in 2010 by Fearless Women Publishing
P.O. Box 6176
Pine Mountain, California 93222
323-874-8500
www.maryannhalpin.com

ISBN: 978-0-615-36719-4

Design: Peter Green Design, Glendale, CA

Story Editors: Dr. Joyce Mills and Gail Speckmann

FEARLESS ACKNOWLEDGMENTS

I would like to thank the many people who helped make this book possible. My heartfelt gratitude to the fearless fabulous forty women who invested in this book project to get it created. Thank you for your trust and support in the creation of this project. Thank you for your full participation and digging down into your souls to share your powerful stories.

A very special thank you to Pam Bush-Davis, our cover girl, who bid so fearlessly on the auction to win the coveted place on our cover. Your generous bid that goes to the eWomenNetwork Foundation will help so many other women and charitable causes that the foundation supports.

Another thank you to the six back cover girls, Rosemary McDowell, Michelle Peavy, Toni Sexton, Peggy Kinst, Deb Greene and Patti DeNucci, who gave their most fearless fiercest bids to win the six spots on the back of the book. Your generous bids will go to the foundation to help so many people.

Thank you for our sponsors, Fine Art Limited LTD (www.fineartlimited.com) for sponsoring Marquetta Glass and Leadership Education Action Program (www.leaptoexcellence.com) for your sponsorship of Gloria Manchester.

Thank you to our support team: photo assistants in Dallas, Brad Barton and Rick Coke; hair/makeup in Dallas, Piper Lincoln; sales assistant and dear friend, Lar Park Lincoln; photo assistants and retouching in Los Angeles, Sherri Johnson and Caroline (Karolinka) Ratajczak; hair/makeup in Los Angeles, Donna Gast and Nicole Bolin; administrative assistants, Michele Basler and Isabella Way; publicity and marketing, Heather Holland.

Thank you to our editors/storytellers, Dr. Joyce Mills and Gail Speckmann, who fearlessly helped all the women dig deep into their hearts to tell their fearless stories. To Betty Liedtke for being another set of eyes and being our human "spell check."

Thank you to Lisa Carrier for her beautiful "Glow Project" candle.

We are so grateful to the legal Goddess and Bond Girl, Sandy Shepard, Esquire, for her fearless legal wisdom and guidance throughout this project.

My thanks to Nancy Alspaugh and Marilyn Kentz for partnering with me on "Fearless Women: Midlife Portraits." Your vision of bringing "Fearless Aging" to the world is a huge contribution. I am eternally grateful for your friendship, support and encouragement.

Thank you to Tim Sims and Bernard Semerdjian for their wonderful design of the book, and to Peter Green for his wisdom and creative guidance, and to all at Peter Green Design.

Thank you to Joe Sohm, photographer and author of *Visions of America*, for sharing his wisdom and being a sounding board.

Thank you to Kim Dower, Kim-from-L.A., for your support and Publicity consulting.

Thank you to my dear friend, Marilyn Tam for your vision in gifting my book to Sandra Yancey. Through the grace of your generosity, and the journey with eWomenNetwork, this book has manifested!

My heartfelt gratitude to Sandra and Kym Yancey for their fearless vision in creating eWomenNetwork, an extraordinary organization that supports women in business and encourages fearless contribution to the world. Our lives changed dramatically when they called us a few years ago to be part of the eWomenNetwork Business Conference in Dallas in 2008 and created the space for "Fearless Women Portraits" to have their beginning. They supported and encouraged me to create portraits for women that have become visual touchstones to remind them of the true fearless women that they are inside.

Thank you for your belief in my work, my message and my art. We are blessed to call you our friends.

Without the love and support of my sweet, dear husband, Joe, I don't think I could fearlessly forge forward in life as effortlessly as I do. Joe is my rock and my heart. He feeds me with his love and his extraordinary cooking. He is a true Renaissance man, videographer, editor, computer guy, pianist, jazz singer and Chef Joe.

You are a brave heart and fearless man. With all my love and with all my heart….thank you!

Finally, thank you to all the extraordinary women who have touched our lives and inspired us to carry the "Fearless Torch." We are grateful for all the women who have joined the Fearless Movement and embrace their sword of courage to help inspire others to move from fear into love.

Introduction

My mantra, my phrase on which I meditate is, "What's your fearless?" I wear it on a T-shirt, and when many people ask me what it means I reply, "I know the question. I just don't know the answer." It has been my mission, to be the fearless messenger. I didn't sign up for this. Or did I?

Fearless lessons are learned in the school of life on planet earth. My most profound lessons come from creating book projects. When I began my journey back in 2003, to photograph my second photo/essay book, "Fearless Women: Midlife Portraits," I walked a path of amazing fear-transforming lessons. Half way through this project, I was rushed into surgery to find I had a tumor lodged in my small intestine. I was told that if I didn't have the suggested two feet of my small intestine removed, I would die within 48 hours. Following my operation, I was ordered not to get out of bed for five weeks. I had to surrender to the reality that I probably wouldn't get the book photographed and completed by the deadline.

A week after I was released from the hospital, I felt a fearless force pulsing through me. Driven by my passion and fearless spirit, my strength grew stronger. Each photo session inspired me to get the book completed. The sword became the symbol of my unconquerable courage, a touchstone to fight the good fight, embrace it and then lay it down in peace. Miraculously, I finished the book with all fifty portrait images of extraordinary women and met the publisher's deadline (or I like to say "life-line").

This new book, Fearless Women, Fearless Wisdom, is once again filled with images and stories of forty extraordinary women entrepreneurs, sisters, mother's, daughters, leaders and light bearers. Regardless of the challenges in their lives, these are women who have risen above it all to lead lives of contribution and inspiration.

This book project began in July 2008, when I was asked to speak on a "Fearless Women" panel at the eWomenNetwork International Business Conference in Dallas. Later that day, I would photograph "Fearless Women Portraits" for any of the women attending the conference who signed up. I was amazed to find out that I would end up photographing 90 women in two and a half days.

Time was suspended as I photographed each woman holding the sword. At the beginning of each session, I would present the sword with reverence saying, "This sword has been held by many fearless women. Now it is your turn."

Most often they would break into tears and tell me the most extraordinary and revealing stories. We would begin by having them connect with their feelings by closing their eyes, taking a breath and focusing on what it was they wanted to say with the sword. It was a fearless dance.

The following year I was asked back to the eWomenNetwork Conference to photograph more Fearless Women Portraits. I also made available Glow Portraits with women holding a candle to symbolize the connection with their inner glow. These images are inspired by The Glow Project Movie created by eWomenNetwork. So, you will see that a few of the women in this book are holding a candle or even a butterfly. My goal was to create a portrait that resonated with each woman, so that when she viewed it on her wall, it would be a reflection of her powerful authentic self.

In this fast paced, fear driven world, I know this book with these forty fearless women will be a true inspiration to others to walk through fear and embrace courage and ultimately live in a grateful heart.

May we recognize the light in each other and live our lives with fearless inspiration. One by one, we can be the peaceful warriors that can change the world.

Yours in Fearless Gratitude,

Mary Ann Halpin

ANNE MARIE HANSEN

Starting "Gianna Homes" at age 26 was a daunting experience, yet it healed my past wounds as nothing else could.

Having been subjected to sexual and physical abuse for several years, I had emotionally and psychologically closed myself off. My parents did not know how to listen to me when I tried to tell them what was happening to me at school. My father was not home much, we were very poor, and children were to be "seen and not heard." When I was seventeen and helping my father, I fell about two stories, landing head first on a cement floor. This "near-death experience" changed my life. I saw a bright light and felt the most incredible peace and love. I knew that God was holding me in His arms, that I had never been alone through all the suffering in my life, and that God still had work for me to do here on earth. My goal became to create a safe place where people, vulnerable with dementia, could be loved and maintain their dignity. I think it has been because of my own pain that I have been able to give unconditionally to those in my care and to my employees.

I came to realize that to lead my staff to be their best, I needed to model an authentic life by first facing my own demons. This was most humbling, but I grew more aware of who I am and why I have acted in certain ways. This took more courage than I ever imagined. As I began to heal, I also began to blossom. Life is not free from pain. It is often life's deepest pain that allows us to see joy.

In our most challenging moments, we see our true selves. Do we crumble or rise to the occasion? Diagnosed with a brain tumor at age 30, I chose to live. Faced with surgery, memory loss and the possibility of being 'terminal,' I reflect on how my own life has paralleled those in my care. I now understand more deeply how my patients feel upon hearing a dementia diagnosis and knowing they cannot change the direction of their future.

I see now that life will pass by if you wait for the big moment ... the right partner ... the perfect job! Choosing to live passionately, I will look back on my life without regret.

Fearless Wisdom:

Fearlessly, and in the face of all odds, I will celebrate life!

Aremita Watson

My life began in one of many small coal towns in the mountains of northern West Virginia. With a life focused on family, my siblings and I were born to a large extended family of ninety plus first cousins. I am a coal miner's daughter, with a legacy of coal dust in my veins. The dangers inherent in coal mining and its associated social and economic implications made fear a constant in our daily lives.

I have always loved music. Music was my conduit for creating stories, dances and songs that were fearless. As an introverted, little brown girl with a strong sense of self and huge intellectual curiosity, I read, dreamed, danced and sang, imagining a life outside of my own.

My life was encumbered with diverging and converging expectations. My life straddled the river, the coal mining town, the white, working class neighborhood integrated by my family, and the college town central to our lives. My mother was a civil rights activist. My father was a union leader. By-products of finding "me" in these relationships were ballooning insecurities, emotional turmoil and paralysis, conflicted, distorted images and messages, and fear of failure and success. While seeking wisdom and direction, I discovered other's secrets of fear, anger, victimization, denial, acceptance, lies and lack of understanding. All were defining elements of my journey of fearless determination.

My relationships, stamped with racial and social realities, sharpened my awareness of manipulated perceptions which dictated the dynamics of my circumstances. Reconciling my reality without total assimilation or compromising my values and safety was challenging. Maintaining my high performance standards, excuses and mediocrity were not an option, while learning skills and tools from each success and failure. My response was a rigid approach to relationships with a hesitancy to trust, even those who cared…a female warrior on a path of self actualization.

Freedom from fear has brought clarity of purpose and vision rewarding me with successes and satisfying relationships. I am empowered to use the tools and skills acquired in my fearless journey to shape rules and outcomes to make a difference. My work with nonprofits provides tools to elevate their level of performance and success.

I challenge each day… to laugh, love, learn and grow… the wholeness of who I am continues to emerge. With my husband, who adds fun and spice to my life, we are dedicated to teaching our daughters and others to seek this fearless freedom.

Fearless Wisdom:

No one knows what song the juke box will play…..use the music to set you free.

Marina Collazo

It is amazing to look back on my life, to see where I started and how the different paths have taken me to where I am today.

I never had a chance to go to college. Instead I started at Hartford Insurance at age 18, and that was my college. I threw myself into learning everything about that business, and I was quickly promoted. When I gave birth to my second daughter, I left to raise my girls. But I was not a stay-at-home mom, so I went into the restaurant business at night. This led to me becoming the marketing and advertising director of a restaurant group. Here I met many business owners, one of whom would change my life yet again.

Hurricane Katrina hit in August of 2005, and I was asked to go to work for a large restoration company, doing sales and marketing. First assignment: New Orleans.… "Restoration 101," you could say! In the next eight weeks my life was truly changed. All of my other jobs were not life altering: this one was. Seeing the devastation that close up tore me apart every day. Every night I cried myself to sleep wondering how GOD could let this happen. The man who hired me was a strong Christian and would email me Bible verses, and at one point he mailed me a Bible. It opened my eyes to see what was really left in this devastation: the strength and fearlessness of the people! I learned from them to always find a silver lining.

With the helpful advice of fellow eWomen members I started my own restoration consulting company in August 2007. I used to say I jumped off the cliff, hoping a boat would be waiting for me. But a good friend told me I jumped off the cliff and spread my wings on the way down!

I truly believe GOD has a job for me: letting other women know that they can do anything and that they should surround themselves with positive people. At the 2009 eWomen conference a lady came up to me and said she had been looking for me all weekend. Though she couldn't remember my name, something I had said to her the year before had changed her life. I had told her to live her life for herself and to get away from negative people. She has since increased her business five-fold and has never been happier!

Fearless Wisdom:

Be positively FEARLESS, sisters, and trust in the LORD that you WILL do great things!

WENDY BIALEK

Ultimately, it is our relationship to uncertainty that determines our path in life. The health of my physical body was my biggest uncertainty, with doctors predicting I would not walk past the age of thirty. My youth was spent mostly in bed, in a wheelchair, or on crutches. Enduring seven surgeries in fourteen years, my constant companion was pain and the fear of permanently losing my mobility.

Amid the darkness of my childhood years were the shining hours spent watching my grandmothers sew and crochet. As I grew I immersed myself in sewing, knitting, crocheting, embroidery, beading, tapestry, basketry, quilting, felt making, and weaving. What began as a way to stay connected to my grandmothers became the magical realm of a new language – fiber.

Intuitively, I sensed how to use the creative process as a visualization tool to "knit" my body back to health. I learned to listen to my inner voice. It spoke to me of turning negative, fearful thoughts into creativity, transforming pain and anger into compassion for others and myself. The colorful world of fiber arts was my lifeline and the blueprint for my life's path.

To sustain myself I wove together an organic wellness approach as my lifestyle, interweaving mind/body/spirit through diet, acupuncture, Yoga, and Chi Kung. I moved to the drier climate of the Southwest, hoping this geographic change would reduce my pain level, which was excessive in the humidity of the east coast. What empowered me as I drove cross-country was a strong belief that I would find a perfect place to live, new friends, and a way to continue crafting my art.

Today I have a partner who loves and understands me and accepts my physical and spiritual journey. Bernie is a wonderful man who made my biggest dream come true – the adoption of our son, Ashton.

We live near the spectacular Continental Divide in Colorado, overlooking a forty-foot-wide labyrinth we created on the side of our mountain. Walking the labyrinth with intention – one path in, the same path out, one step at a time – focuses my creativity and grounds me spiritually, weaving together the elements of my many experiences within this magnificent tapestry called life. Uncertainty? One thing I am entirely certain of is that the unknown path ahead is what makes us grow and is ultimately a blessing.

Fearless Wisdom:

Embrace uncertainty with fearless intent, weaving the threads of your experience into a vibrant, colorful tapestry that reveals the unique woman within.

TONI SEXTON

High school dropout at 15. Unmarried teen pregnancy at 16. Homeless with a baby at 18. Victim of physical and mental abuse well into adulthood. This was my life…not a promising start!

Today, at 42, I am the CEO and founder of a successful healthcare company with a six million dollar payroll, an adult son who shares my entrepreneurial spirit, three more beautiful young children, and married to a successful attorney.

Trying to regain control of a once-hopeful future after my turbulent teenage years used to be a painful process. But with each passing year, each struggle overcome, and each challenge met, I discovered that I was resilient and that my life was an adventure. The lessons learned became part of the fabric of who I am today, who I will be tomorrow, and what I will be remembered for when my children think of me.

When I first started the business – it was on a wing, a prayer and the goodwill of a special client who believed in me. We couldn't afford equipment. Instead, I showed some friends pictures from a catalog, and we made the equipment. That equipment and that special client are still part of our business today.

Recruiting good talent is always a challenge when you are the underdog. Fourteen years ago, I met someone I really wanted as part of the company. But she had a management position with a stable and large corporate company – and was breadwinner for her family. It took me almost two years to convince her to join me in building this vision. But she fearlessly took a risk on me, left her corporate position, and for 10 years now, she has served as our Director of Operations for the therapy division. I am proud to say that my company and client list are filled with fearless women who each have remarkable stories.

There is no time for fear. There is only time to take action against that fear and make decisions that will take you down new paths of experience and learning. Whether right or wrong, painful or joyous – you build on your experiences, embrace the mistakes, and enjoy the successes. Somewhere along the road, you realize that you are capable of choosing the direction of your life.

Fearless Wisdom:

No matter where you are on your road, FEARLESSLY carve out the path ahead.

DEB GREENE

In August of 2009, I felt this photo was my "coming out" event. After being in a life-altering car accident in March 2005 my life changed in an instant. While stopped at the bottom of a freeway exit ramp, my car was rear ended at approximately 65 mph by someone playing with their cell phone. I found myself struggling with the simplest of tasks. Even more devastating, I was questioning my identity and how I would ever get my life back.

A "Triple A" personality, I had a successful real estate practice and was very involved in local, state and national organizations. I thought I had everything "calmly under control." In the blink of an eye I was immobilized. I was deep in denial, struggling physically and emotionally with excruciating pain. Recognizing how impatient I'd become, I prayed for God to open my heart, mind and soul to all possibilities.

In the past my "Iowa work ethic" had seen me through many tough times, but I realized that this was the biggest challenge I'd faced. Trying to survive from minute to minute, the isolation, constant pain, and mind-numbing drugs began to take their toll.

I found inspiration from new friends at the "Courage Center" who had survived much worse, and was blessed with many unexpected friends who stepped up to help me. Refusing to believe the negative reports saying that my physical health had been permanently damaged and that I might not be able to work again, I was determined to recreate myself.

Along my healing journey I discovered a new resolve and strength. But first I needed to let go and let God lay out His plan for me. I needed to constantly remember while I grieved for my lost health, the "footprints in the sand" were not mine walking alone, but rather God carrying me.

I played a game with myself of "if I could do anything, what would I do?" I contemplated my strong and weak points (normally my neck). As an optimist, laughing at the odd things that happened during my journey helped me keep perspective. But I still needed to remind myself of the factual limitations which I might be faced with. I reprioritized my life, did research online, called associates in different businesses, ran some ideas by trusted friends and kept working hard at rehabilitation.

I am still growing, still glowing, and continue my commitment to improving life.

Fearless Wisdom:

With faith and humor, the unpredictable challenges in life may become our greatest blessings.

MARQUETTA GLASS

Just when I thought my career life was cheating me, I was embraced by God's Grace in my corporate office. It was there that the test of the human spirit met with a spiritual sword. The idea of entrepreneurship and creative innovation was in direct conflict with a corporation that was having its own culture clash with outside pacesetters.

Realizing that many business societies are overwhelming, I envisioned an environment that would be harmonious with the enterprise. As a champion for others and for exceptional performance, I needed to create a portal for spiritual collaboration that would allow me to conduct business, while decreasing pessimism.

It was at this point that I remembered seeing a Bible in the United States President's office. I thought if the Bible could be in such an important place, certainly my office could benefit. I decided it was time to nurture my soul and bring God into my workplace. I began by reading my favorite scripture daily. I released the political conflicts and experienced optimistic environmental changes. My colleagues saw my office as a positive place to discuss new ideas and share their views on a Higher Power in their lives.

As I began to experience the spiritual freedom of my soul in the corporation, I achieved a new profound confidence. My passion for bringing joy to others gave me courage to seek a larger vision that would prove to shape the minds and hearts of millions. Using faith as my confidence cornerstone, I invited our CEO and the people's poet, Maya Angelou, to tea. A true treasure, her words stir the heart, giving hope and love to those willing to participate in the human experience. What magnificent creative victories my soul embraced on that day. That tea party resulted in a multi-million dollar brand.

Today I am a global business woman and speaker, rejoicing in the wisdom of Dr. Angelou and her sister-friends, all passionate vessels who transitioned through the adversities of their day and became the eagles that soared. I am grateful to my corporate leaders for the standards of excellence. I am empowered by women and the universal, mothers and daughters in my life today who carry their own individual swords. Their gifts of spirit represent golden beams that continue to light my path daily. I have learned to rely upon God in all situations, using prayer as my anchor and joy as my sword.

Fearless Wisdom:

Become a life-giving spirit and release the limits of your
"ego soul" by seeking a spiritual "Higher Power" daily.

JEAN CARPENTER-BACKUS

I was an orphan, a high school dropout and never finished college. I was married at 14, had a child with birth defects at 15, and at 16, joined my husband who was stationed in Germany. Six months later, due to abuse, I flew back to the States with the clothes on my back and a small suitcase for my son.

My starting point: no home, no family, no education, no money, no job, no driver's license and no legal ID. A child psychologist pointed out these harsh realities and suggested I give up my son for adoption. It was a gut wrenching decision. I was counseled that my son would be adopted by parents that had the means to provide for him in ways I could not. I came to believe that it was the most loving thing I could do for him.

Where am I now? I am happy, grateful, I've had three wildly successful businesses, I am blissfully married, and I am wealthy. I'm the author of The Naked Accountant Asks: Who's Standing on your Financial Hose? as well as a public speaker and teacher.

You would think by my starting point that I was screwed, right? I'll tell you what happened. Angels in the form of people started showing up. They taught me compassion not only for myself but for others as well. No one gave me money except for the Red Cross - $25/week for a month. My vow early on was to become an angel myself and give back...pass on the compassion, generosity and kindness that others selflessly taught me. Ironically, my gift showed up in the form of helping women overcome financial anxiety. After a 30-year career, I know this is my calling because it does not feel like work, it is my passion, it makes me smile and it helps others. I am clearly a messenger.

Fear can be debilitating and does not discriminate based on wealth, status, or place in life. Once you navigate past fear, you are greeted with a liberating clarity that enables you to build a yellow brick road to financial freedom. I help women navigate past this fear using the lessons I learned from creating my own yellow brick road. It is authentic, fun, unorthodox and provides relief. It has never failed. I teach women to look anxiety in the eye and say, "BRING IT ON!"

Fearless Wisdom:

No longer an orphan, I feel like a princess and I'm honored to give back. Coming Full Circle...Priceless!

Patti DeNucci

Two months before this portrait was taken, I was sitting in church witnessing my son's Confirmation. He had chosen Michael as his Confirmation name in honor of St. Michael, the Archangel who brandishes a sword, courageously fights evil, and bravely escorts souls to Heaven. It was a fitting choice for our teenage son who is determined, strong, and fearless.

How ironic that the next morning I'd receive news that my father was dying and probably wouldn't last the night. By some miracle, I made it to Dad's side just hours before he passed. My sister and I held his hands tenderly as he took his last breath, remembering what a caring father and extraordinary person he had been. In that surreal moment, we prayed he was at peace, feeling love, and experiencing a welcoming light, bells pealing, angels singing, and God saying, "Well done." Despite wrenching sadness at the loss of my last surviving parent, I remembered St. Michael was close at hand. All would be well; I had nothing to fear.

A sense of divine providence filled me when weeks later I learned about Mary Ann Halpin, her book, Fearless Women, and the opportunity to have my portrait taken holding her mighty sword. Surely this experience was being presented to me for a reason. What a fitting way to honor my father and son and to claim my own fearlessness as I continued on my own life journey as a woman, wife, mother, writer, solopreneur, and creative spirit.

As Mary Ann handed me her sword and snapped this special portrait I felt renewed love and confidence. It was a personal confirmation reminding me that not only could I be, but I must be fearless in my faith, life, relationships, and work.

Since then, I've taken on a bolder and more determined attitude, as well as a new project I've wanted to do for nearly 10 years, but was somehow afraid to begin: my first book, a field guide for solopreneurs. I'd always known I would write a book, but had struggled with uncertainty about what to say and whether anyone would be interested. Those fears still emerge from time to time, but quickly melt away. The work is too important to me now. My desire is that my book serves as a source of wisdom and inspiration to others, just as my father, son, St. Michael, Mary Ann Halpin, and her sword have served as inspirations to me.

Fearless Wisdom:

Being fearless means facing, and then accepting in your heart and soul, who you are - and who you are called to be.

DEBBIE HOOVER

The year before my 50th birthday I began to wake up to the woman I was born to be. For the first time, I felt mental connections, intuitions, more compassion toward others, and love for myself. Up until this time I had been living in a "dream-like" state, numb to all of my feelings. I created this numbness so that I didn't have to feel the emotional pain stemming from my childhood. I matured physically at a very early age before most of the other girls. This led to constant bullying leaving me to feel different, ugly and unlovable. I desperately wanted to fit in.

That was then and this is now. I decided to create a new mantra to help me put into practice what I wanted in my life. Every day I said, "I am going to be fit, fabulous and 50!" From then on, I began to notice changes in my life. My body began to "shift" and I was becoming more shapely and thin. I truly was redesigning my body, not only through my thoughts and words, but also by choosing to eat smaller portions of wholesome foods. I learned to "make love to my food" and truly enjoyed every bite I put into my mouth.

My confidence began to improve in all areas of my life. Gifts were coming to me in many ways like new friendships and opportunities. I began to practice spiritual disciplines such as silent meditations, fasting and prayer.

My awakening is continuing each and every day and I know God has a greater intention for my life. I believe my Divine Purpose is to be an example to others about the power we each possess to create the life we truly want to live. This is an amazing journey and time of my life. I know I am a powerful woman and can do anything I choose to do. Yes, there has been pain and tears along with laughter and pleasure. My heart and soul are truly awakened. It is so good to feel alive again. My gift to each of you is to know that it is safe to wake up to the woman you really are meant to be in life.

Fearless Wisdom:

Remember sometimes you must embrace your fear, walk with it, feel it, and maybe even learn to love it in order to discover your lessons and let it go.

PEGGY KINST

Sometimes blessings present themselves in mysterious ways!

When I was diagnosed with ulcerative colitis, my dreams of becoming an English literature professor were replaced with a lifelong search for health, happiness, and spiritual awareness. The road was not always smooth. Each medical challenge and surgery made the journey of becoming a "Wellness Educator" and president of my company, Target Health Systems, Inc., that much more difficult…that much more urgent. The personal challenges – surviving my divorces and coming to terms with the "rules" I had stubbornly adopted to be the perfect "everything" – made the journey of becoming a compassionate but assertive woman more necessary. The dichotomy between the masculine and feminine roles, as I saw them, became more confusing. Was I the "masculine" persona of my creative father/ entrepreneur or the "feminine" counterpart of my sweet, nurturing mother? Knowing now that I can be both, I honor whoever I am at any moment in time – a mom, a lover, an entrepreneur, a woman, a child, an educator, a student of life, an evolving spirit – I strive to love them all.

As I look back on my 62 years, I feel so blessed to be where I am, having the guidance to paint the dreams of my future! I am on my path – a continual, sacred journey of learning and sharing what I have learned. My fondest achievement is the Wise Women's Journey to Inn-Lightenment, that I host every year. I believe I am here on this earth to bring people together to share, to heal, to celebrate ways to reach far beyond whatever was thought possible – to say, "I believe I am worthy to accomplish great things…personally, professionally, financially and spiritually."

Being "Fearless," and holding the sword, symbolizes to me my place of inner strength, my sacred place filled with a passion for living life to its fullest. My prayer is that everyday I will open my heart to love and forgiveness, be awakened by the beauty and joy surrounding me, be attentive and humbled by the lessons from the messengers God sends me (thank you, dear sons). And also, I must remember: when I laugh, it feels like champagne bubbles exploding through my body. Life is too beautiful to be too serious and not to enjoy every bubble!

Fearless Wisdom:

Jump fearlessly into the current of God's blessings and be carried joyously to a place of peace, passion…and wonder!

Linda Lee Kaye

Growing up in the South, any relationship with my father required me to understand and obey the rules of a man's world, dominated by the values of the 1950's.

My mother, victimized by those same rules, had been afraid to break them and lost her dreams. As early as eight years old, she took me aside and ordered me to break out of the mold. I promised that I would.

Predictably, I learned to operate well in a man's world, becoming competitive, tough, smart and strategic. There was no room for fear or weakness! I closed my heart, watched my back, and kept my distance. Neither happy nor fulfilled by age thirty, I realized that something had to give. It turned out it was me that had to change.

In 1980, I moved to Southeast Asia and lived there four years. For the first time in my life, I had to confront living outside the comfort, convenience and the context of our American culture. I had to become responsible for what it means to be a citizen of the world in the midst of complex political and economic challenges. To say that it changed my life would be an understatement. I woke up.

I became passionate about my own and others' transformation. I adopted a new set of rules to live by:

- Regardless of fear, I must stay the course. Fear is an emotional state that's useful. It's a powerful signal that I'm out of my comfort zone and in breakthrough territory.

- At any moment in time, regardless of circumstances, I get to say how my life is going to go. I can take a stand and make something happen rather than continue reacting and adapting to the existing state of the world I'm in.

- Thinking is the driver of everything. If I don't have the results I want, I must figure out what thinking had me taking the actions to produce that result. I can choose something else, take a different path.

- The more attached I am to any outcome, the more I have to lose. For me, this is THE source of fear. I must get unattached and play full out for the outcome anyway.

Fearless Wisdom:

Fearlessness comes from consciously converting fear into power to become alert, awake, alive, and able to act!

SAMI DOUGLASS

My husband and his secretary are missing again!
Both boys have the flu, and the dog has it too
Laundry, groceries, and cooking to do…
What in the world am I gonna do?
I've stayed at home, done each job, large and small,
lost myself for what I thought was "having it all!"
Being the shadow behind the successful man,
now doesn't feel like the best-laid plan.
Scarred and scared, I will try harder,
but in the world will I ever get smarter?

What do I want, what do I need,
where will I go, where should I flee?
I know very little, my skills are but few,
who am I to think I could start anew?

Lost in the life of being a wife,
looking for growth inside of a box,
tied to a washer that eats up the socks,
I must change the song, for this one feels wrong.
I've had enough of following along.

Love songs are always what speak to my heart,
I will write one now and make a new start.
Do I remember how to love ME?
Surely I do! Yes, surely I do!
That is the answer to starting anew.

I leave fear behind, gone with the old me,
but what in the world is it I could be?
First, I must have compassion, a kind, loving heart
for someone so brave as to make a new start.
Love myself, I must! so I can move on,
That is the main verse for this new song!

How do I love ME, feeling worthless and alone?
I think it would be easier to play the trombone!
Clarity, focus, belief, and grit,
are the answers for getting myself out of this deep pit.
I see hope on my face,
I feel strength in my heart…
YES, I am ready to make a fresh start!
I call upon courage and the support of friends,
offer my forgiveness and start again.

Do what you love! That's the entrepreneurial way…
the answer for the success that I enjoy today.
I discovered a new and beautiful me,
who has run FIVE, not just one great company!
Who would have thought life could be so giving,
I just needed to love ME and start true living.

Fearless Wisdom:

Living a life with all the love in my heart,
was the fearless answer to make my new start.

VICKI LYNN KLASELL

From a very young age my father had always told me, "Never pass up an opportunity." What I have learned through the experiences in my life is that opportunities are not always what they appear to be, nor are they so easily recognizable. They often come disguised as challenges.

One challenge in my life has been having a baby with respiratory problems. At eleven months, my son Trenton required regular nebulizer breathing treatments at home. By the time he was two and a half he needed treatments every four to six hours. Trenton was suffering and was a very sick little boy. With his need for round-the-clock attention, his care was emotionally and physically exhausting for me. Finally, Trenton's Respiratory Specialist recommended that I stop the use of all chemically-based products in my home; he wondered if that is what was triggering Trenton's asthma. I followed his advice and converted my home to chemical-free cleaning, laundry, and personal care products. In only three weeks, Trenton no longer required breathing treatments on a regular basis.

Trenton's miraculous turn-around inspired me to research the vast array of medical problems caused by chemicals in our homes and especially to our children. The information and results I found absolutely shocked me. I knew I wanted to get involved so that I could help others make healthier choices about the products they use, thereby making a difference in the lives of children and their families.

This experience completely changed my life and my career. Along with spending seven years in medical sales, I am a Registered Nurse. Inspired by my son's asthma, I now run my own successful health and wellness business. I have partnered with a manufacturer of consumable products which are healthy, safe and eco-friendly. In addition to saving money by ordering directly from the manufacturer, my customers receive palpable health benefits for themselves and their families. I am passionate about what I do. It is so rewarding helping others who are dealing with health challenges. I do not just earn an income; I am able to change lives.

I really do believe that everything in life happens for a reason. It is up to us to figure out what the reason is. Some of the greatest challenges in life can be turned into opportunities through your positive attitude, faith, courage, passion, and persistence.

Fearless Wisdom:

Within our own mind, we determine the height of the mountains that we must climb.

39

"I don't know!" ... and ... "Nothing."

These were my answers to the questions I was asked when I decided, in my early 50's, to follow my dream of becoming a professional speaker. Questions like, "What's special or unique about you?" "What are your qualifications and credentials?" "What do you do, or know, that will convince people to hire you?" I suddenly realized how ordinary my life was. I had a husband, two kids, and a dog. I'd had a full-time job before the kids were born, but only part-time, freelance, and volunteer work since then.

I coped with breast cancer right after my second child was born, and then with severe heart damage from chemotherapy. I survived my kids' teenage years, and the farewells that came all too soon as my son went into the Marines and my daughter to a school and a new life 1500 miles away. These gave me a world of life lessons and experiences, but didn't make me unique.

Then, at an "Inspiring Speakers Workshop," I met two women who had been violently assaulted, and who now wanted to speak out in order to help others. I was in awe of their courage and the realization that in uncovering and exposing what they had kept buried inside themselves, they would also be recovering and reclaiming their own strength and confidence.

"It's like digging up buried treasure," I thought, and was suddenly struck by a lightning bolt: There's buried treasure in everyone. Even...me!

What really makes each of us unique are qualities that come so naturally to us that they don't feel special at all. And our "credentials" include the wounds and scars that have also become a part of our identity. From this wisdom my company, "Find Your Buried Treasure, LLC," was born. Through my writing and speaking, I help people discover gifts and talents they don't even realize they have, and ways to use those gifts to enrich themselves and others. In 2009, I became a Certified Dream Coach®, working one-on-one with clients to help them discover their own buried treasure and how to use it to fulfill their dreams. I love working with "ordinary people," and also those who feel lost, broken, or in need of healing. These are the people who are going to change the world...as soon as they realize they can!

And in helping others find their power, their passion, and their purpose, I've discovered my own.

Fearless Wisdom:

Being fearless means following your heart, discovering your strength, and never giving up on your dreams.

JULIANN KELLEY

I remember bringing home a report card that had all A's and one B. I was so excited! When my father saw my report card he said, "Great job, but what happened? Why the B?" He was looking for excellence. From that point on I always feared that I would never be good enough. Anything less than perfection would not suffice.

Over the years I have been a disc jockey, a private detective, a mortgage broker, an event planner, and now a handbag designer. I have followed my passion and listened to my inner voice. Always striving for excellence, I moved past my fear of change to try something different.

There was a voice inside of me that often said, "You can't do that, Juliann." But I would do it anyway. Amazingly, it stopped telling me "I can't" and started encouraging me that "I can!" I learned, "Don't be afraid to challenge your inner voice."

I made my choices, but not always did I like the road that I was on. Sometimes the road was very hard and uphill. I continued to make changes as I followed my passion. Oftentimes I was told that doing this was too risky. I knew I might have to take some risks, but I didn't have to risk everything! And even so, good things can come out of difficult times.

In order for me to be successful, especially when working in male-dominated careers, I felt that I needed to overachieve. In reality I learned that all I needed to do was "give it my best shot," be myself and work hard. I knew that I could compete and work with them by following my passion. I learned, "Don't be afraid to step up and say, 'I can do this!'"

While running my private detective agency, I became frustrated with the work and with my employees. I found myself expecting the same perfection from them that I was expecting from myself. Ironically, my father was the one who helped me through this. He said to me that when I expect excellence I need to accept "great" or even "good." Excellence will come. It was at that moment I understood, "Why the B?"

I challenge myself to put fear of change and of not being good enough behind me. I value being able to laugh and have fun. I would rather try, taking a chance with making a change, than always having to wonder "what if..."

Fearless Wisdom:

Fearless women turn the negative voices that they hear from themselves and others into something positive, and look for the lesson that they offer.

Louise Griffith

As I reflect back upon my life, I realize that even as a child, there were things that I knew within my soul, even though I didn't have specific details.

My parents separated and divorced at the time I was beginning high school at the Academy of Holy Angels. I had loved my freshman year! When my mother told me during the summer that I could not return due to finances, I was both devastated and very angry.

Consumed by these feelings, I went to my "soul place," Lake Harriet. As I walked around the lake, experiencing the warm sunlight and fresh air, a feeling of calm and peace came over me. I knew within my soul I would be going back to Holy Angels. I returned home to tell my mother that I was going back to my school and announced that I was going to get a job. I was just 15.

Even though I was very enthusiastic as I walked into my first store, I was told that I was too young to work there. Choosing to not feel defeated, I knew that there would be a way. On my second stop, a neighborhood drug store, I decided that I would tell my story straight from my heart. I had seven wonderful years working there.

My school provided me with many leadership opportunities which enhanced my life and contributed to a scholarship for college, where I earned my degree in elementary education.

An important lesson was imprinted within me at that time to pause, quiet my soul… listen, listen, and listen some more. When the "knowing" comes, I can proceed through the open door, even without specific details. It has served me well to listen and pay attention to the intuitive insights.

Intuition led me to pursue a Master's degree in Counseling Psychology at the Adler Graduate School in my mid 30's. Finances were tight as we were raising our children and sending them to a private school. My soul knew my next bold step. I applied for a student loan, something I had never done before! And now, I love my work as a psychologist, coach and speaker.

Fearless Wisdom:

If you don't honor your own soul, who will?

LAR PARK LINCOLN

I had heard the phrase, "This Too Shall Pass," but it was just a saying, it didn't have any meaning. Acting for 30 years, in film and TV, and being a regular on Knots Landing, my life felt golden. Then my husband and parents died from cancer at young ages. I lived through a severe earthquake and the stress of being stalked for six years; I felt it was enough trauma for anyone to bear.

A single, widowed mother, I raised two children. As an on-air celebrity host for the QVC Shopping channel, I was traveling constantly. It was a dream-come-true when my first book was published. Holding more than one job since I was 15 years old, I was always busy, too busy. At 47 I was tired and needed to make changes. The Universe decided to make them for me.

Diagnosis: Breast cancer. A biopsy two years prior was benign, but a gut feeling told me it wasn't. When the lump was causing so much pain I could no longer ignore it, I went in.

Stage Three. Treatment: Surgery, Chemo, Radiation. I thought reconstruction would heal the trauma. It didn't. It brought a whole new set of issues; uncomfortable implant reconstruction that doesn't look or feel like normal breasts.

Regardless of my actions or lack thereof, life kept going day by day, without any help from me. Problems solved themselves. I didn't rush to appointments or rush to do anything. Nothing was so urgent. Life took care of itself.

I was not pain-free or energetic, but as each hour, day, week passed, the phrase "This Too Shall Pass" kept humming in my mind. I prayed the nightmare would pass. It did, excruciatingly slowly.

I realized that it wasn't just bad times that passed; it was good times too. "What was the point of getting well if the good times also passed?" With the importance of this phrase in mind, I had rings made for my children inscribed with "This Too Shall Pass."

I suggested they twirl the ring during difficult times, knowing that if they let life work its magic, things would be okay. I told them to twirl the ring when they were happy; to accept that all things pass, good and bad. Now I'm peaceful in the knowledge that all things pass, and I will be okay.

Fearless Wisdom:

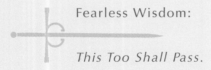

This Too Shall Pass.

DEBRA DION KRISCHKE

My passion is helping women with no voice. This portrait, stunningly, sums it up.

Having lived in the Middle East for 2 years, it is hard for me to even call myself a "Fearless Woman" when I think of women enduring the kind of oppression that I have seen. These women exemplify true "fearlessness"… the ability to fight on behalf of your mother, daughter, sister, or girlfriend, and do so at the peril of your own life, day in and day out! Being defiant, even respectfully and quietly defiant, can cost you your life. They are fighting for the right to work so that they can feed their children. They are fighting for the right to attend school, to walk about in public without a male escort, to have their voices be heard, to choose their own spouse… to live without fear! I feel a tremendous calling to show solidarity with these women and share their message, using my own voice, for those that cannot speak. The women in the front rows of this revolution show courage beyond compare.

This portrait represents them all, in a way that words never could.

Fearless Women Under Veil. There, but by the grace of God, go I.

As a special event producer for women's initiatives, I will continue to seek out methods for raising money and awareness to support women with no voice, locally and globally. With laser focus, I trust that the universe will unfold opportunities for me to be most effective. My job is to steadfastly keep moving forward in health and intention.

Fearless Wisdom:

When your passion is fueled by your heart, the universe conspires to assist you.

GLORIA MANCHESTER

I believe that God directed me on a path to become a fearless warrior for children and women.

Sometimes events in our lives are so compelling that they alter our course and define our purpose. I was born the youngest of three girls in a French-Catholic community in Canada. As a child, I lacked for nothing. According to my mother I always shared my food and toys, and I had a heart for gathering less fortunate friends. One of those defining moments in my life occurred when I was five years old. My best friend was one of twelve children whose mother had abandoned them. One day I walked into her house to play and saw the father naked and on top of her. I ran home confused…and the image never left my mind. My mom called the police and the children were taken away by Social Services. I was heartbroken… I had lost my best friend.

Years later, I gathered a group of powerful women leaders to participate in a retreat. The intention of getting together was to champion a cause. At this event, we discovered that seven of the eleven women had been sexually abused as children. I went on a mission. Out of this event I co-founded CARTE (Child Abuse Resolved through Education). In this same year my teenage cousin disclosed her sexual abuse to the family and I took temporary custody of her. It was through these experiences that I recognized the enormous damage caused to children by sexual abuse. In 1991, I collaborated with Rosalie Gibbons, MFT and Dr. John Gray, author of Men are from Mars, Women are from Venus, to create the first STARR (Succeed through Accountable Responsible Resolve) Program for Teens. This program has served thousands of lives touched by sexual, physical and emotional abuse. Today CARTE provides an experiential therapeutic program for abused teenage girls and victims of domestic violence… transforming their scars into stars.

I am a spirited entrepreneur with many projects going at one time. I am the President of Leadership Education Action Programs and a personal/professional life coach, one of few certified in Emotional Intelligence (EI) Coaching. I have developed and facilitated leadership seminars for over 25 years. In this work, as in my life, I set a context with my own practiced words; "Fear is the distance between the thought and the action."

Fearless Wisdom:

As a compassionate and fearless warrior, I offer up the sword… challenging others to join me in being a bold interruption in healing the wounds of child abuse.

PATTI LUSTIG

In 1975 I was 27 years old and had just graduated from the University of Florida. Not being sure of much of anything in my life, I decided it was time to step out, take some chances and start living my life fully.

I stuffed all of my earthly belongings into every nook and crevice of my tiny '65 Volkswagen Bug and set out on a 3,000-mile journey to California. It was hot; I had $80 in my pocket, no air conditioning, a loaf of bread and a jar of peanut butter and jelly, the phone number of an old college roommate, and a thirst for adventure. That's about it. I was not going for anything or anyone specific. I was just moving forward.

I made it to Los Angeles in about a week. Each day something new unfolded. I saw places, met new people and had experiences I've treasured my whole life. As I look back on it now, I remember that I almost turned back a few times, because I was afraid of being alone and failing. The thought of not having anyone or anything to back me up was terrifying, but I pressed on. Each time I doubted, I remembered the wisdom that a good friend had given me just before I left: "Believe and trust that what you need will be there when you need it."

More than thirty years later, the spirit that was there in 1975 is still fully alive in me today. That trip shaped my whole life.

I have overcome and continue to move through many fears in my life, allowing me to fulfill my dream of being a powerful, professional woman who has made an important and positive difference in the lives of thousands of people.

Trusting the universe and myself has allowed me to be successful personally and professionally. I taught emotionally disturbed teenagers and managed the operations of an international, multi-million dollar training company. Presently, I own and manage a one million dollar portfolio of real estate, and run a successful consulting and coaching business. Not to mention being the mother of an extraordinary daughter and marrying the man of my dreams.

As I move through the second half of my life, I am filled with excitement and anticipation. I look forward to the adventures that lie ahead, and I continue to be moved and inspired by others who are making their dreams comes true.

Fearless Wisdom:

Joy comes from jumping in and living life fully. What are you waiting for?

Pamela Bush-Davis

I was a teenage bully – fighting, cussing, and intimidating students and teachers. School paddlings and suspensions meant nothing to me. Nothing bothered me except seeing my mom strut up the sidewalk to yet another meeting with the principal.

I don't know why I had such a combative attitude. I had friends, I exceeded in athletics, and my grades were good, though I rarely studied. My parents were solid people and strong disciplinarians. But I was headed down a path of self-destruction and unfulfilled promise.

Then it happened. Friday night at a football game I was my usual bullying self and called my teacher a disrespectful name to her face. I soon discovered I'd crossed a line. Monday morning found me back in the principal's office with my parents, but this time there was no suspension – I was expelled for the remainder of my sophomore year and had to attend an alternative school for troubled students. I remember little of what was said, as I was overcome with shock.

My punishment had escalated to a higher level. For the first time, it was I who was frightened. I'd been the "bad girl" at my school. Here, I found out what "bad" was and felt literally scared straight. These kids were mean and non-caring. I was looking at myself in the mirror and did not like what I saw. It wasn't who I wanted to be. Immediately, I began to turn myself around.

After successfully finishing my sophomore year, I attended a vocational school where I was exposed to kids who cared about grades, about their future and about each other. Following graduation I completed a nursing degree and eventually started my business: Advantage Claims Recovery Group, Inc. (ACRG). Today I am CEO of a thriving business, have my soul mate for a husband and many wonderful friends.

There are two things I know for sure. First – we can change, sometimes dramatically, no matter what age. Perhaps a difficult and fearful experience is what it takes to make that decision. It did for me. Second, I know I have a Creator who wants the best for me always. There are times I don't recognize His presence in my life, but He's there nonetheless, no matter what. He loves me and He'll never forsake me. That knowledge makes every situation an opportunity for a fuller life, knowing that together with God, I can fight through every fear and win.

Fearless Wisdom:

When I consider the various aspects of my life's journey, the obstacles as well as the opportunities, I'm reminded that the Key was always in me.

ROSEMARY MCDOWELL

Three words that best describe me as a "fearless" woman are Persistent, Resolute, and Committed. I have worked through numerous obstacles to reach my lifelong objective – the financial security and independence to devote myself to things I love – my family, my work, and my causes.

With persistence and sheer fortitude, I survived an abusive marriage reminiscent of The War of the Roses, a 14-year child custody case totaling hundreds of thousands of dollars, and questionable business decisions. Despite the obstacles, I resolved to never give up. Within days of foreclosure, extreme debt, and chronic depression, the sword came into my life at what was to be my lowest point. Every time I felt the end was near, I touched my sword and it reminded me of the strength within, the ability to go on, and how lucky I was to have a supportive husband and network of understanding friends.

I am committed to having a strategic plan in place for my business, family, and charitable causes, so that I can assess where I am and where I'm going. For example, I've learned to have a clear course of action that states how much I will give to each charity rather than blindly giving out $10 here and there. In today's fast-paced world, it is critical to have a plan for your family; otherwise precious time can easily slip through the cracks, especially with your spouse. My weekly Sunday Brunch with my husband opens our lines of communications, we know where we stand, and we seldom argue. We both know what our family guidelines are and agree to them. Our marriage works! Being committed to a working plan ensures satisfaction for my business, family and causes.

The candle symbolizes the GLOW that came into my life as I was coming out of the depths of despair from financial ruin. My sword represents my ability to survive and thrive. Today, I am an accomplished speaker and presenter on Federal Government contracting for small to mid-size businesses communicating advice on marketing, proposal, and pricing strategies. My business runs itself, my financial situation is strong, and my personal life has come together. I am the strong-willed, determined, and energetic leader who people count on to get the job done no matter the obstacle and, most importantly, a woman respected by her peers and her family – this is my true definition of success.

Fearless Wisdom:

Fearless – overcoming adversity with a smile.

ADRIENNE McGILL

While contemplating my "Fearless Portrait," I thought to myself, "What am I fearless about?"

My business reflects my passion – lingerie, beautiful things, and helping women. I am a bra fit specialist, intimate apparel stylist, and sensuality educator. Every day I meet women who are terribly critical of their bodies. According to them, they are too fat, too thin, too busty, too flat, too saggy, too-- too-- too! And the descriptor is not very nice. A lot of women that I meet think they can't wear a pretty bra and panties set until they look perfect or until they find the perfect someone for whom to wear it. I always say, "Don't wait, because I wish I had the body I had 20 years ago and in 20 years, I will wish I had the body I have today."

I decided to put my money where my mouth is. I asked Mary Ann to take my portrait in my bra and panties, with the idea that I would hang the portrait in my store. My hope was that, as women looked at my less-than-perfect body, they would have the courage to embrace their own. I want to help each woman feel good about herself and enjoy being womanly. My portrait is meant to send this message to women – all women! "Don't wait to wear something you really like...stop being so hard on yourself! What we see in the media is representative of a very small segment of women and, most likely, it is not very real. Embrace who you are today. Enjoy the present! Look, we all have room for improvement but if you focus on what you hate about yourself, that's all you are going to see!"

Finding the courage to hang my portrait in my shop has been for me a journey in fearlessness, all by itself. At times, it's uncomfortable. I wonder what people will think of me. It's a constant reminder for me that it is okay to be myself and that some of the things we fear won't hurt us at all.

My obsession with lingerie started while working in corporate America. I used to wear pretty lingerie just to help me feel like a woman. I worked in a male-dominated industry and was around men all the time. I wore the prettiest lingerie under my boring navy blue and black suits. No one knew but me. I felt like it gave me my power – feminine power!

Fearless Wisdom:

Fearlessly enjoy being the woman that you are!

Joyce C. Mills, Ph.D.

At seven I danced on stage at Carnegie Hall. At 13 my father disappeared from my life. I became a tough teenager with failing grades. At age 15 I was a regular on Dick Clark's American Bandstand where my future husband paid a dollar to join my fan club. I married him at 19, and in 1967 our first son was born with cerebral palsy." He changed my life forever becoming my "hidden angel," to find my life's purpose – psychotherapy, writing and speaking. My soulful philosophies embody the butterfly's transformational spirit and an inner sword of fearless faith.

On February 17, 2009 those beliefs were severely shaken by a serious confrontation with my own mortality. Preparing for a business luncheon, I suddenly felt like a knife was ripping my stomach open from the inside. Hearing me scream, my husband immediately rushed me to the nearby hospital.

An IV was started, and a procedure was initiated with reassurance that it would reveal the problem. I was completely unprepared for what happened next.

When I awoke, I was hooked up to oxygen and delirious from pain that was searing through my body. Diagnosis: acute pancreatitis with life-threatening implications. Something completely out of my control was happening to me, and I was terrified. Overcome by physical weakness and emotional turmoil, I literally felt my life force slipping away.

For three weeks I read inspirational books, prayed, and was visited by loved ones and spiritual healers. I was sent home with orders to rest and not work. Four weeks later I returned to the hospital for a successful surgery. From a medical perspective I was cured, but my core self knew that I was not healed.

Tumbling through emotional darkness and imprisoned by fear, I knew my soul had to be liberated . . . but how?

The answer came with the help from my spiritual brother with whom I participated in many ceremonies facilitated by Native American healers. I desperately needed one now. During the ceremony flashing images of the love, care and prayers I had received from so many inexplicably fused together into feelings of joyful renewal. I felt transformed; reconnected to my source of inner strength.

Today, I know the gift of my illness is a metaphor for the challenges that will continue to arise throughout my lifetime. By staying connected to my heartfelt belief in the power of living in fearless faith, I can face any adversity with courage, wisdom, and the spirit of determination.

Fearless Wisdom:

Fear is the Messenger, Faith is the Message.

LORI PALM

Who am I? What am I here to do? I had become what I thought everyone wanted me to be and in the process I lost me, and so the adventure to find me began.

Two years into the journey, many things in my life were uncertain. I had left a 25-year marriage. The lease was up on my apartment and I didn't know where I would live. I wondered if I would ever find my soul mate. My consulting business was surviving, but money was tight. I was in doubt about my future, questioning what would happen to me.

While co-facilitating an experimental workshop on passion and purpose in the Yucatan, magic happened. Knowing it was time for a break, I decided to take a walk along a deserted tropical beach with my companion. Unexpectedly, I felt a powerful desire to find a conch shell. Seeing the shell clearly in my mind, I knew exactly what I wanted but really didn't know why.

After walking for some time, I began to lose hope, seeing there were almost no shells on this beach. Frustrated, I declared, "I would be happy to find just the center spiral of a conch shell." Suddenly, I looked up and saw two men walking towards us wearing business clothes and shoes-definitely not dressed for the beach. As they approached, one of them pointed towards the water saying, "There, that's for you!" As I moved closer, I saw a large, totally whole conch shell about eight feet into the water. I waded in, picked it up, and showed it to my companion. I turned around to thank the man only to find they were both nowhere in sight...they disappeared. In that moment I knew these Guardian Angels had been sent to me with a message-"Reach for what you desire." I now believed I was a co-creator of my future, ready to take the next step and expand the scope of my business.

Through the years, every time I looked at the conch shell I wondered, "What else do I need to know?" It was if it was spurring me on to find a deeper meaning. Once again an answer came when an Aztec dancer was placed on my path and told me the conch shell is the messenger. Now holding the sword, the message of Passion, Power and Purpose continues.

Fearless Wisdom:

When you know WHO you are, you know WHAT to do.

MICHELLE PEAVY

Once upon a time, I was minding my own business, when all of a sudden life got in the way. Unforeseen circumstances happened to two dear friends that changed the way I looked at life forever. One had a quadruple bypass, went into diabetic coma, lost her eyesight and could not walk. Four months later another friend was hit by a car while riding her bike and is now a quadriplegic. Even as I write, my heart beats just a bit faster.

From the day I found out what happened to them, I really started to appreciate just how valuable life is and how it can so quickly change and be taken from us. Prior to these events I was on what I call the "Freeway of Life," driving too fast and not paying attention to all of the signs. These tragedies taught me how to get off the freeway and pay attention to my life.

Each day as I watched the ordeal of my friends' recovery, I dealt with intense anxiety. Because it was all so close to me, I found myself inwardly questioning "Was I next?" As I looked closer at each of their experiences, I received unexpected gifts of insight. While one friend could not see or walk, she used her intuitive mind and voice to make positive things happen. Unable to walk, eat, or even use the restroom on her own, my other friend continuously inspired me to see what she could do, instead of what she couldn't do. I realized that even with the use of arms and legs, we can feel disabled.

Through all of this, I learned that life is too short, and WE MUST LIVE OUR DREAMS AND DO WHAT MAKES US HAPPY. Happiness is the key.

What makes me happy? I have a gift of singing since I was a little girl. The blessing I received from the tragedies of my two friends is to do what I love – sing. My mission is to touch people by singing to their souls. Singing opens the soul to the songs within the heart. Some of us keep our talents hidden deep inside, never getting the chance to experience true happiness.

Ask yourself this question: What would I do to be happy, even if I knew I wasn't getting paid to do it? Whatever answer you come up with is your passion. Give voice to your passion and sing.

Fearless Wisdom:

Do what you love and love what you do. Just do it!
Never give up on what you LOVE.

MARY PIKE

Growing up with an alcoholic mother and an Air Force father was a lonely, frightening experience. I went to three high schools and had my first date in my senior year. Because of limited interactions with other teens my age, I thought I was in love with the first guy I met. Three months after graduation we were married and he joined the Air Force. The marriage proved to be getting out of the frying pan straight into the fire.

I truly wanted a happy family and having a baby seemed the logical next step. Arriving five weeks premature by emergency C-Section, my tiny baby girl had life-threatening complications. Her first bottle caused her to choke and her heart to stop. Ultimately, a hole was found in her esophagus causing the milk to fill her lungs. She was the first baby less than three pounds to survive that surgery.

My marriage decayed, as nothing I did for my husband was good enough. My life was scripted, caged by fear and a nightmare. After 18 years, and another daughter, I summoned the courage to get out.

I had been enhancing my own nails for years. Realizing I was very good at it, I got my license, opened a small nail salon, and helped women restore self-confidence while making their nails beautiful. Business soared, expanding into a full service salon. Both my daughters worked with me through high school. My oldest continued for 27 years, building the salon into Blushes, the largest Destination Spa in Granbury, Texas. She assumed ownership, continuing the tradition of dedicated service. Besides the salon, I built a successful western store, pet shop, car wash, Laundromat, and locksmith business, and eventually sold them.

I married a loving man who helps me enjoy the life I never had. My youngest daughter is married and the mother of my fabulous grandson. My oldest daughter survived her health challenges and now has a perfect daughter.

In the past five years I've taken a passionate interest in health and nutrition, teaching others how to correct the damage done by unhealthy environments and toxic food choices. At 62, because of my nutrition, I look better than I did at 40 and feel better than I did at 30. I am driving a beautiful copper Corvette and take Ballroom Dance Lessons. Life can definitely be better in the "Golden Years" and I want to share that philosophy with the world.

Fearless Wisdom:

You are what you think. Think yourself Beautiful and Successful and you WILL achieve it.

Paoola Sefair

Fearless wisdom.....what can I possibly share about being fearless?

After all, not a day goes by that I don't experience some type of fear. That's right – flying, public speaking, to name a couple of big ones. As I reflect and search for inspiration to share with you, it hits me: fearlessness is ultimately experienced when – regardless of being fearful – you face the challenge head-on. You sign up for projects that will require lots of public speaking, knowing that every time you get up there, you will probably feel like a few years were taken off your life! Okay, maybe I am exaggerating, but you get my point. Or you get a job that puts you on a plane 90% of the time. Yes, that's right: 90% of the time! Why?! Why do this to myself? Because the day I allow my fears to rule my life is the day I stop living fully. It is the day that I deny myself wonderful, fascinating experiences – the moments in life that are worth remembering.

One of these memorable moments that comes to mind is during one of my trips to South Africa. I had the chance to drive around the slums of Johannesburg and the opportunity to meet with local women. I got to hear their stories first hand, the challenges and obstacles they faced every day! And it made me realize not only how extraordinarily blessed I was, but that I had the responsibility to do something to help.

The awareness gained through this experience set me on a new path, one that has led me to participate in and create several projects benefiting women in other countries. This experience changed my outlook on life – to think I could have missed out on this because of fear!

Unfortunately, I don't think there are any shortcuts, magic spells or quick fixes that eliminate fear. I've searched high and low. The answer I always come back to is very simple – just do it! I know it's easier said than done and can be quite a daunting task. But if accomplished, it can lead to the most gratifying, exhilarating, uplifting, spine-tingling experiences.

Fearless Wisdom:

The day I allow my fears to rule my life is the day I stop really living.

SANDY SHEPARD

Hey there. I'm Sandy Shepard. Mary Ann took this portrait to show that I stand ready to cut through the crap clients have drawn into their lives. (She used roses though. Nicer visual.) I'm an attorney, a coach, a wife, an author…a worrier, a couch potato, a procrastinator. My passion is helping "reverse-engineer" seemingly impossible dreams into mission-driven goals with doable action steps. And – by tying these goals to a charitable purpose – I show folks how others' hopes and prayers can help pull their "impossible" dreams into reality.

My life has been like one big Wedding Vow: Sometimes richer, sometimes poorer…sometimes in sickness, sometimes in health…sometimes better, sometimes worse. You, too? Well, if you're at a poorer/sicker/'worser' time, the psychologist William James says: "To change one's life: Start immediately. Do it flamboyantly. No exceptions!"

Earlier this year, I felt I had to change my life. How to do it "flamboyantly"? I needed something extreme and impossible…something with a completion date, action steps… something where accomplishing my goal would benefit others. So instead of getting in bed and pulling the covers over my head (well, maybe after a little of that), I started training with the Leukemia & Lymphoma Society's Team-In-Training for the Louisville Ironman® triathlon: a 2.4-mile swim, followed by a 112-mile bike, then a 26.2-mile (marathon) run.

When I started training, I hadn't worked out in three years. I couldn't run a block. Now, a few months later, just before sitting down to type this, I ran for an hour after biking for an hour.

Why go for this goal? I believe, as the Roman poet Juvenal wrote, that a Sound Mind (which I needed) only exists in a Sound Body (which I definitely did not have). I picked something flamboyantly outrageous – a body-thing for a mind-girl – because if I can do this, I can do anything. Oh – and help cure cancer, to boot.

So, be flamboyant in a time when folks are being so freakin' fearful. Turn your passion into a goal with action steps, a goal that will bring hope to others when you accomplish it. If you're using your God-given sword to file your nails: Stop! Go out and brandish it.

Fearless Wisdom:

Fearlessness is pulling on your big girl panties and getting on with it, even if your knees knock.

70

GAIL SPECKMANN

I was a good caterpillar. I put one foot ahead of the next, ahead of the next, ahead of the next…

Oh yes, there were times when my feet attempted to move in all directions at once. Imagine where that got me … Nowhere! My flights of fancy excited me, but also left me confused. So instead, I feasted on the experiences the world offered. Filled, yet unfulfilled, I became simultaneously anxious and lethargic. This almost unbearable combination became so great that all I wanted to do was die. I even spun my own shroud and crawled inside.

But I was impatient for death and dealt myself a mortal wound. Shockwaves of alarm sounded throughout the butterfly kingdom. Ministering "angels" with particularly tender hearts and gentle wings hovered about my disturbed cocoon, where I remained for a very long time. But with the loving nurturance of my butterfly angels, I healed and grew in understanding. Finally I emerged, with wings so strong and brightly colored and decorated with the diamond tears that had been showered upon me.

> **Emergent butterfly, your untried wings still wet,**
> **Poised and hovering on the precipice of possibility.**
> **No way back. A fearless flight forward**
> **Your only salvation.**

As I took flight, I knew my mission. I understood far more about difficult transition for having been through it. My intended death had become instead a hard-fought birth, an initiation into the band of those who seek out the troubled ones to offer them hope, the sure and certain promise of transformation.

Artist, poet, author, wife, mother, daughter, sister…Child of God! When the storms came, I forgot my true identity. With deeply confused mind, I believed that "I will not live like this!" meant that I had to die. Having long walked the razor edge between passion and despair, this time I attempted to take my own life. I burrowed deep inside a blue sleeping bag and cut my throat. (Four years later, with amazing irony, Mary Ann photographed me tenderly holding the blue butterfly and wearing the "transformed" sword at my neck).

The subsequent guidance I sought and received gave me strength and purpose. My art and writing are dedicated to helping those who are in their own "dark nights", those who are in their healing process, and those concerned "angels" who are hovering in love around the wounded ones. My book, **HAVE HOPE! Sharing the Journey from Suicidal Depression to a Healed Life** will offer you this message of…

Fearless Wisdom:

Fear Less.   Trust More.   HAVE HOPE!

Patti Waterbury

For 20 years as a single, career-focused woman, I traveled all over the world working with business leaders to improve results and help people develop the skills to master change. In 2002, challenging circumstances forced me to use those skills to re-evaluate everything and make a series of decisions that forever changed my life.

After pushing myself beyond the limit for over a year, I successfully culminated the biggest assignment of my career. Although it was a high point in my profession, I was exhausted. While exploring options for my next assignment, personal challenges mounted. My mom was diagnosed with terminal cancer. Since she was the primary caretaker of my five-year-old nephew, it became necessary to balance my work with caring for my mom along with learning how to be my nephew's "heart mommy," as he liked to call me. Within two years, life as I had known it was over. I went from being a single professional to being a single mom, losing my biggest cheerleader and lifelong friend when we buried my mom. After three major surgeries that left me in constant pain, I was unable to work. For several months I didn't know if I would ever be able to put two thoughts together, much less work again.

The fear I felt was paralyzing. If it were not for my son, I would have given up. Powerless and angry at God, deep inside I knew that I didn't have the strength to recover without His help. During an intensive healing process I worked through my anger and pain, regained my ability to function, and reconnected to my faith in God's love. Believing in His strength helped me overcome my weakness. I learned to trust Him in spite of my questions. Eventually, I returned to work; however, during my absence my reputation as a valued contributor and one of the best consultants in the company was overshadowed by the question, "What have you done for me lately?"

As I reflected on how quickly accomplishments can fade, as well as on the impact I wanted to have, I knew more change was in order. I eventually left the company and formed Creative Growth Strategies, Inc. to help Kingdom-minded leaders grow and use proven practices to increase business profitability and attain wealth for Kingdom advancement. It's been an incredibly satisfying journey. I have learned to never give up!

Fearless Wisdom:

Always have Hope, believing with God's help you can rise above any situation you will ever face.

Jacqueline Wales

Fearless....The 'F' word has held a lifelong fascination for me. As a child growing up in Scotland I was raised in a violent, chaotic household with a raging alcoholic father. I learned very early in life to run for cover. My earliest memories are of tears, which were understandable because I was either ignored, yelled at, or smacked. Growing up, my life became a mirror of the behavior I saw at home. Alcohol, drugs, and abuse became my story. Self-esteem was something that other people had.

By my mid-twenties, I had been busted for drugs, left home at 16, given up my daughter for adoption at 20, married at 21 and left my son with his father when I was 25. At age 35, now in a second marriage, and pregnant for the third time, I made a decision that would change my life.

This child would leave me before I would ever leave her.

It was time to figure out why I had spent the years running away from life, because this child's life depended on it. In order to do that, I would enter the fires of hell and truly become the phoenix that rises from the ashes.

It has now been twenty-two years since my daughter was born. In the interim I also gave birth to a third daughter and raised a stepdaughter who arrived on my doorstep, a complete stranger at the age of 10, from Thailand. All of my children, including my son and adopted daughter, are healthy, vibrant, independent people whose lives are filled with love. It is no small testament to the power of healing.

Over the years, I have learned that in order to be truly fearless you must show up to face the fear. I made choices that confronted my fears, and refused to run away, deny, or hide. Becoming fearless was an obligation that I owed to my children and myself.

At age 58, I understand completely that overcoming the fears of oppression, low self-esteem and habituated negativity is critical if we are to live vibrant lives. Facing my fears has given me the opportunity to experience the many blessings of strength, courage, and wisdom that I now share with others.

Fearless Wisdom:

I believe that being fearless is not the absence of fear, but it is the choices and decisions we make when fear shows up in our lives.... That is what living our best life is all about.

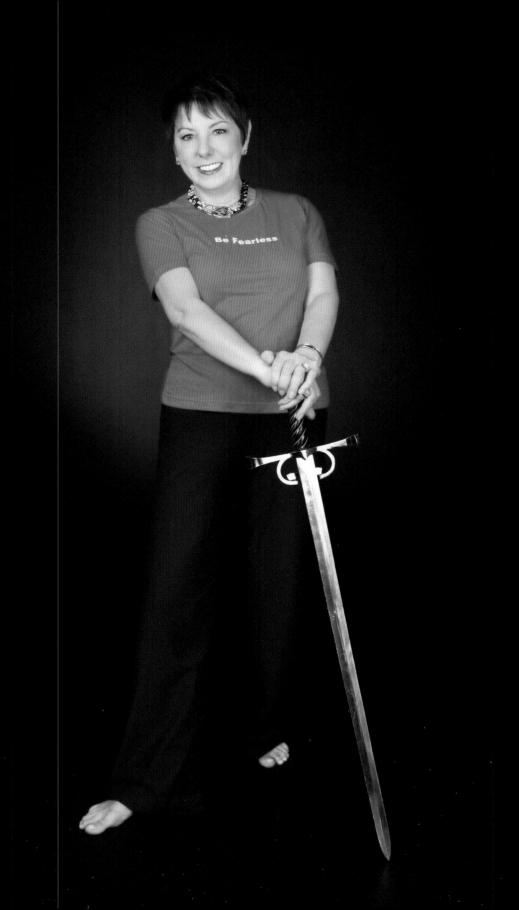

JENNY TELWAR

In the past 12 years of my life, I have gone from being a college graduate student (working three jobs, eating spaghetti four dinners a week, and watching only one channel on the television because I couldn't afford cable), to becoming the wife of an entrepreneur, mother of two, and a successful CEO of an international company. This company, America's National Teenager Scholarship Organization, was purchased creatively through sheer determination, hard work and without a bank loan. During these years, I gained a lot of "life titles." "Life titles" are what I call the different roles women juggle most of the days of their lives.

Adaptability to each life title, along with the joys and challenges each encompasses, is what I believe makes a woman a fearless being and a powerful force on this planet. With each title in my life, comes the daily "fearless lessons" of patience, trust, openness, resilience, "out of the box" thinking, and perseverance.

My life titles have brought me a wide variety of experiences over time, along with a myriad of emotions, both positive and negative. Always, there is something that I have been taught. I have come to see that learning the lesson, even the hard lesson, and facing head-on the challenges associated with it, can be empowering.

Being who I am, exactly who I am, at all times, with all these life titles, is extremely important. I do not compartmentalize each area of my life into the models or patterns I feel fits those titles. My question is not "How is a Wife/Mother/CEO supposed to act?" but "How does Jenny feel and see this situation?" And finally, knowing where I am going AND how I am going to get there, is more invigorating to my day than any cup of coffee.

Being clear on who I am and what I want to become are the keys to making my authentic existence a reality. Taking the challenges and facing the changes involved....These are taking steps in a fearless direction. And so my path continues...

Fearless Wisdom:

Living fearlessly is living authentically.

78

KARNA SUNDBY

When I was 42, I felt that I was living a "charmed" life. I had just landed a brilliant job with a thriving Fortune 500 company, had finally met the man of my dreams, and was blissfully living with him in a cozy beach house on the Puget Sound. Those dreams died when I came home from work one November evening to find his unresponsive body. He had ended his life. I could almost hear the sound of my future shattering as the medics carried him away. The support of family and friends, counseling, and a deep spiritual connection brought me through that first devastating year of sorrow. I learned so much about how my body, emotions, psyche and spirit had internalized the trauma and, also, how to process and let go of the grief. I considered becoming a grief counselor to help others survive their losses in life.

Then I learned of NLP (Neuro Linguistic Programming) which is the study of the human brain and the way it stores our life experiences, emotions and beliefs. I began a journey of embracing the vast array of resources within myself, not only to heal, but to grow and discover more strength, compassion and depth than I had ever known. The path to healing was profound, as I learned to feel my emotions without fear. It was completely transformative as I grew so much beyond just surviving. Life, itself, became so precious, and all the ways in which I had grown were such gifts. They helped bring meaning to my life and changed my perspective on death.

As I became grounded in gratitude, I realized that I wanted to help others beyond just surviving their pain. I wanted to help people access their own inner wisdom and experience transformation in all areas of life.

Today I have created new dreams that I am sharing with my wonderful husband of eight years. I am passionate about my coaching business where I guide people to deeper insights for brighter outcomes. This sudden tragic death in my life led to my greatest transformation. I believe that our most difficult challenges and fears can give us an opportunity to discover our greatness and embark on a journey of becoming fearless. When I help others on this transformational journey to find the healing and the gift in their challenges, I know I am fulfilling my own life's purpose.

Fearless Wisdom:

Becoming fearless and compassionate are the gifts we receive when we disrobe our fears, claim our power, and trust our inner guidance.

KARIE WOOD

Looking back on my life, I recall my mother telling me that I was strong and could do anything. I was 9 and had a 3-year-old brother when my mother brought home another newborn baby brother from the hospital. My father left us for the first of many times, the last of which was on my 16th birthday. Money was scarce. My mother and I both worked hard and took care of the boys. We moved often; I went to 10 schools in 12 years, always the new girl. Fortunately, I made new friends easily.

In 1963, at age 20, I gave birth to a baby girl. I made the very difficult decision to give her up. A year later, the State of Minnesota called to let me know my child could not be adopted. She had mental and physical problems and was not expected to live past 5 or 6. I saw my blonde, blue-eyed, 13-month-old daughter. I held her in my arms, and then I had to go before the judge to ask that the State care for her. I had not known a darker time in my life.

Life had to go on. I applied to be a stewardess for Northwest Orient Airlines and was hired! Traveling the world… what a life it was! At 30, I met Jon, a pilot for Northwest. We married, and I acquired 2 teenagers and a dog. Life was good, but trouble followed. My drinking became out of control, and I was taken to a treatment center. Last December I celebrated 30 years of sobriety.

On Mothers' Day 1984, my own mother saw a newspaper article. It told of a young woman graduating from high school, whose greatest wish was that her mother could see her accomplish that feat. That young woman was my daughter. She had no mental problems; her limited sight had led to a slow development. When I came to her door, my daughter Mary and I stood face-to-face after almost 20 years! We hugged and cried and started our life journey together.

Retiring from Northwest after 40 years, I then started my own company, Lifekare. I had been dealing with asthma and fibromyalgia. The Wellness Company had all natural products for taking care of my home and myself. I find it very rewarding to be able to set up accounts for people with the excellent Melaleuca products that they carry.

When Mary Ann handed me this sword, I felt calm and powerful. I could see my life, through each difficulty and pain, fearlessly recovering and going forward.

Fearless Wisdom:

Fearless, I awaken each morning and choose that this day will be good.

TERRI STARNES-BRYANT

President of an international company, happily married, five children, three grandchildren, lovely home...

My life has not always looked like this, but I have kept my heart open and made courage my choice... through some of life's toughest challenges.

I am Terri Starnes-Bryant from High Point, North Carolina. For the past three years I have been president of Microtronic US, LLC, based out of Switzerland. Microtronic has been in business for 25 years providing "Cashless/ Contactless Technology," mainly to the vending machine industry, and offers the best "in-house" system on the market today. I was given this opportunity after repeatedly approaching Microtronic Switzerland. I, along with my sales team, have been awarded distributorship for North and South America, Canada, and Australia.

There have been numerous businesses that I have started in my lifetime, attempting to find the perfect match. I have tried and failed, but never refused to try again. In 1988, I came to work at "Columbian Coffee & Vending Service," starting as a warehouse and office worker. I worked my way throughout the company, from stocking, driving the tow motor, counting the money, to becoming the full-time bookkeeper. I later married Steve Bryant, who at the time owned "Columbian."

I have a son and a daughter from my first marriage, two stepdaughters, and a daughter that I had with Steve after a reverse tubal ligation. I lost my first husband to suicide; I had a heart attack at age 45. In 2007 my home of 16 years burned to the ground, due to a chimney fire. I have fought many battles with family drug abuse, but my faith and perseverance have kept me going.

If there is one major life theme from which I have learned, it is that I have tried and failed and tried again. I do not like to accept failure, but have experienced that failure can happen. I have found that it is what you do with each situation that makes you the person you are. You cannot let the circumstances around you control you, but you can learn from them.

Fearless Wisdom:

Be the most positive, optimistic person you know,
and NEVER give up!

Susan K. Younger

When I was young, my mom used to say, "Honey, being painfully shy, smart and tall, is not a combination people understand. You'll be mistaken for stuck-up. Learn to reach out to people. Make them comfortable in your presence. Have a sense of humor and common sense."

Along with the sense of independence my parents instilled in me, these words of wisdom served me well as I moved away to follow business opportunities. Finding myself in cities where I knew no one, I remembered to reach out to people. I started to make friends through coworkers, neighbors and other business associates.

After 25 years in architecture and retail design, building and remodeling department stores, I wanted to create a business for myself. Massage therapy had been an interest, but not something I thought I could build a career on when I was younger. In my 40's I found a way to work it in around my other profession.

When I said I was taking classes in massage therapy, people would ask why. I always replied, "Now I can run away with the circus." Either they understood I wanted independence or they were so confused they thought I was joking.

After several years, I was still working 80-plus hours a week in someone else's business, while marginally having time to develop my own career. It felt like I was determined to be either worn out or fired. Sometimes it takes being kicked out to realize it's time to move forward. I heard God and the universe say, "OK, here's your chance – now make it happen."

August 2001, even though I was on a desperately thin financial shoestring, I knew I had to cut all ties with the other job and stand on my own. There was no time for worry. With a trusting, optimistic attitude, I moved forward. I built a strong client base and took care of their needs.

Today I take care of myself by getting sleep, gardening, and enjoying everything, no matter how small. I seek out the glory of everything. I invite friends over to enjoy simple meals and their company, making a party out of nothing. Connections support me emotionally, physically, mentally and financially. I don't get sucked into drama. I know life is too precious and it is important to savor every moment. I feel more alive and connected to my life than ever before.

Fearless Wisdom:

Honor your connections and they will honor you.

SHERI' TABER

I am a fearless advocate to so many, something I never had. A legacy response to an eight-year-old's account of sexual abuse, "Never talk about it again and do not cry," would be indelibly engraved in my soul. "You didn't talk about these things in the 1960's." Heeding the order for silence, I paid the consequences for many more years.

Longing for a "Father Knows Best" lifestyle, I married young and was heartbroken when abuse repeated in marriage. Promises to bankrupt me and leave me longing for my children, empowered the "do not tell, do not cry" canon for twenty years.

I found an advocate in a gifted counselor who helped me break the cycle. I claimed my voice, my life and my independence.

A litigious divorce awarded my husband every asset in my name and forced me to assume 100% of the family and business debt to win custody of my three young children. Broken financially, but not in spirit, I embraced the opportunity to be an example of strength and to share my story about the freedom and power that are available when one embraces her inner power and shatters the bonds of silence.

I am quintessential proof that anything is possible. In addition to putting my children through college, I have been a finalist for several local, national, and international Businesswoman of the Year awards, including the 2009 Tampa Bay, eWomenNetwork Businesswoman of the Year. I am the CEO and founder of a global performance management consultancy supporting the successes of hundreds of organizations.

My message of hope, strength and triumph over adversity is palpable. I have personally inspired thousands of men and women to empower themselves, heal their hearts, achieve their purpose and pursue their passion. I am a passionate fundraiser and serve teens and those who are affected by abuse through my affiliation with community and national organizations.

My motivational and inspirational creed is: "What I've done wrong is eternally forgiven. What I've done right has the potential for generational healing and achievement. It is the profound consequences of what I'm supposed to do that I have not done that tenaciously compels me forward."

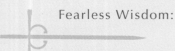

Fearless Wisdom:

I learned early on that in the darkest of times, clearly and without exception, the immediate and magical antidote was to serve another.

Ruth Thoes Vivrett

Growing up in Wichita Falls, Texas, in the late 40s and 50s, my parents always said there was nothing I couldn't do if I just tried. Taking this lesson to heart, it evolved into my favorite saying: "It's all good!" This phrase means there is something to be learned, felt, and experienced in whatever challenges come my way – and come they did.

My first layoff in the mid-90s was devastating and left me questioning my identity – I realized I had so much tied up in titles and accomplishments rather than who I was. The gift: I traveled around the world, meeting incredible people and seeing places I would have never seen. My second layoff found me better prepared for the emotional rollercoaster of losing a job. The gift: I took the life experiences I had gained and started my financial advisory business. Helping my clients achieve their financial dreams is awesome, and doing it while working for myself is the best. But I had more to learn.

In July 2007, I was diagnosed with breast cancer. Hearing the words was terrifying, as I had lost my older sister to breast cancer in 1992. She chose to keep living life fully each day she was given, so I knew I could do no less. My husband and I decided there would be no half-measures in treatment -- we chose a double mastectomy, chemo, and all the surrounding activities. He kept our treatment notes, asked great questions, held my hand and found ways to make me laugh even when there was little to laugh about. I worried that I would lose my business, my appearance, and my love of life. Well, I did lose my hair for awhile and my figure (no reconstruction for me at my time of life!), but my business actually thrived and my love of life is even more firmly engrained.

Until this experience I had not really considered how many friends I had made over the years, and yet they were the ones who just showed up to carry us through the tough times. To this day, our gratitude remains overwhelming for their love and support. Thankfully, I am still cancer-free.

Each morning when I get up and put feet to the ground, I say to myself, "It's all good – take advantage of whatever you are blessed to receive and get on with it!"

Fearless Wisdom:

Despite your fear, take action and deal with the results of that action.

TO MY WISE AND FEARLESS FRIEND

CONTACT

Anne Marie Hansen | Gianna Homes | p.12

Gianna Homes-Sursum Corda is a ten bed residential care home. We demonstrate a unique understanding of memory loss and the challenges it creates for our residents and their families.

We are dedicated to preserving the dignity of an individual while providing for his or her medical, social and spiritual needs. Our care is given in a home designed to honor God, nurture family, and foster friendship.

4605 Fairhills Road East, Minnetonka, Minnesota 55345
952.988.0953 | 952.210.8836
anne@giannahomes.org | www.giannahomes.org

Aremita Watson | The Aremita Corporation | p.14

Non-profits struggle with a resource trade off between services and maximizing business performance. The Aremita Corporation, a financial management solutions firm, liberates non-profits to focus and execute their core mission through strategic needs based budgeting, funding acquisition and improved accounting, operational processes, management controls and technology.

Silver Spring, Maryland
240.305.6292 | aremita@aol.com

Marina Collazo | Restoration Coalition | p.16

Flood restoration for commercial or residential properties nationwide. A C N telecommunications Videophone, local & long distance, wireless, satellite & home security for commercial and residential properties nationwide.

630.805.0651 | 877.805.0651
marina@marina-marketing.com | www.marinac.acnrep.com

Wendy Bialek aka "Wendy the Weaver" | p.18

My textile studio offers unique wearable art and one-of-a-kind fiber art pieces for residential and commercial interiors. Your involvement can be direct or long distance, your choice. Also offered are guided group labyrinth walks and events. Creativity workshops are available for those wishing to discover and express their inner artist.

1630 A 30th Street, Box 606, Boulder, Colorado 80301
303.443.1234
wendy@wendytheweaver.com | www.wendytheweaver.com

Toni Sexton | Fusion HealthCare-CEO | p.20

Fusion HealthCare is a privately held company, with a focus and emphasis on patient-centered care and excellent customer service. We currently service 7 counties surrounding the Tampa Bay area and are in the process of expanding our service area to include Sarasota and Hernando counties.

2511 West Virginia Avenue, Tampa, Florida 33607
toni@fusioncare.net | www.fusioncare.net

Deb Greene | Deb Greene Delivers | p.22

~ Minneapolis, MN

REALTOR, ABR, CIPS, CRS, ePro, GREEN, SFR, REEA

Deb Greene is a REALTOR with Coldwell Banker Burnet, Author & National Speaker/Instructor. Her speaking style has been called fresh, enthusiastic and as an "EduTrainer" enlightening!

866.300.0777
Deb@DebGreene.com | www.DebGreene.com

Marquetta Glass | MGS Innovations Group | p.25

We specialize in branding concepts & strategies, licensing partnerships, bridge funding, social media /multicultural marketing, and coaching. Interactive presentations include: "Business Mapping Leverage," "The Genius of God in the Office," and "Unmasking Your 'Ego Soul.'" We will reconstruct your business model to generate long-term global business solutions and greater value.

816.665.2841 | 816.304.5144
mglasses7@sbcglobal.net | www.mgsinnovationsgroup.com
Sponsor: Fine Art Limited LTD, www.fineartlimited.com

Jean Carpenter-Backus | Carpenter & Langford, PC and The Naked Accountant, C.P.A, C.F.P. | p.26

Our CPA firm handles complex tax issues, preparation & planning. First I had a job, then a 30-year tax career & now I have a calling. As The Naked Accountant, I am a public speaker, author & teacher. I help women find their unique financial identity by moving past their fear.

Austin Hill Country, Texas
512.913.3157 | 512.795.0300
jean@carplang.com | tax-rx@austin.rr.com
www.thenakedaccountant.com | www.carplang.com

Patti DeNucci | DeNucci & Co. | p.28

Writer/Author, Speaker, Connoisseur of People Who Make an Impact, Professional Connector, Advisor to Freelancers & Solopreneurs

5114 Balcones Woods Drive, #307-430 Austin, Texas 78759
512.418.0527
patti@denucciandcompany.com | DeNucciandCo@aol.com
www.denucciandcompany.com
www.denucciandcompany.com/denotations

Debbie Hoover | Back on Track! Solutions | p.30

Back on Track! Solutions provides systems and solutions to get you and your company focused, organized and productive. We do this through workshops, one-on-one sessions and seminars. Small to large companies, corporations and institutions benefit through our trainings.

6801 McCart Avenue, Suite A-2, Fort Worth, Texas 76133
817.797.8364 | debbie@backontracksolutions.com
www.backontracksolutions.com

Peggy Kinst | Target Health Systems, Inc. | p.33

As a Wellness Advisor, I search for the most innovative programs available to empower people to make healthy life decisions. Some of the tools I incorporate are the MBTI (Personality Preference), Emotional Matrix (Harnessing Inner Power), AFLAC, Financial Self Reliance (www.financialsr.com), to Create Wealth, and Leave a Legacy.

Oakbrook, IL 60523
Office: 630.916.9677 | Cell: 630.926.5827
peggykinst@helloworld.com

Linda Lee Kaye | The Right Writer LLC and LTC Financial Partners LLC | p.34

Freelance writer and author, Linda Lee Kaye writes transformational stories and books for children and articles on long-term care protection. Also an Independent Agent in the Long-Term Care Insurance industry, Linda Lee specializes in long-term care protection for women and small to medium-sized business owners in seven states.

610.608.3388 | lindalee58@mac.com
www.therightwriterforyou.com | www.ltcfp.com

Sami Douglass | Sami Douglass, Results Coach | p.36

Creating "YOU" Coaching

I'm in the business of Love. Love your life, your self, your choices. As a motivational speaker and results coach, I help individuals identify, clarify, and simplify, making room for what and whom they desire, and love. You will see life-changing results, and create a life you love.

314.406.5470
changeswsam@yahoo.com | www.samidouglass.com

Vicki Lynn Klasell | The Wellness Company | p.39

I help people improve their health. I focus on Asthma, Allergies, ADD, ADHD, Autism, skin problems, and auto immune disorders. I have partnered with a manufacturer of consumable products which are healthy, safe, and eco-friendly. I set up accounts so consumers can shop direct, ultimately saving money on consumable items that they are already buying. Additionally, they receive health benefits, and are making consumer changes which are better for the environment.

Prior Lake, Minnesota
Office: 952.226.4664 | Cell: 952.836.8684
Vicki@klasell.com | www.VickiLynnKlasell.com

Betty Liedtke | Find Your Buried Treasure, LLC | p.41

I am an author, professional speaker, and Certified Dream Coach®. My mission is to help people discover their strength, embrace their power, and achieve their greatest dreams.

Chanhassen, Minnesota
612.743.1488 | betty@findyourburiedtreasure.com
www.findyourburiedtreasure.com

Juliann L Kelley | Juliann Diva Collection | p.42

A distinctive collection of sassy, blingy, knit handbags designed to be as unique as you are. They're fun, fresh, and offer women a chance to stand out from the crowd and be "her own unique self." Every design infuses an element of handcrafted style. The exclusive, beaded handles add a bit of sparkle and set bags apart from other designers.

Design, manufacture and sell hand-knit handbags that are as unique as you.

856.419.1155
Juliann@julianndivabags.com | www.julianndivabags.com

Louise Griffith | One Shining Light | p.44

Louise helps YOU get clear about what you want–and achieve it. Under her spirited and practical guidance, YOU learn how to access YOUR power and passion, build new strengths and break free from challenges. Louise, an international speaker, psychologist and SUCCESS coach works with clients and companies who want more!

952.484.3100
Louise@oneshininglight.com | www.oneshininglight.com

Lar Park Lincoln | p.46

Lar's coaching is focused training for actors and speakers. The goal is to master the complicated audition ,and to effortlessly perform, under difficult conditions. She trains the performer to use proven technical skills to shine on camera!! *Get Started, Not Scammed* was written to guide Hollywood hopefuls from falling prey to those bent on separating future stars – and unsuspecting parents from their hard-earned cash. She also provides guidance for all the marketing needs to promote an acting career. Lar guided her own daughter to win Miss Texas Teen, and her pagentry coaching has netted quite a few crowns!

972.596.9283 | www.talentstart.net
www.larparklincoln.com | www.getstartednotscammed.com

Debra Dion Krischke | Team Effort Events and Foodie Fundraising | p.49

Team Effort Events is a special event production company dedicated to producing events to increase awareness and funding for women's initiatives. Their website offers tips and expertise that can help anyone producing events, from Grassroots to Galas!

Co-author of *Inspired Entrepreneurs – a Collection of Female Triumphs in Business and Life*. Founder of The Burka Project. To make a difference for Women in Afghanistan, check out the matching funds available through the "I Am Powerful" campaign. www.Care.org

Pittsburgh, Pennsylvania
724.935.6100
Debra@TeamEffortEvents.com | www.FoodieFundraising.com

Gloria Manchester | Leadership Education Action Programs (LEAP) | p.50

CARTE-Child Abuse Resolved Through Education (501C3)

LEAP provides personal/professional development and team leadership courses and coaching. All LEAP course fees support the nonprofit CARTE and the STARR Program, a self-esteem building curriculum for abused teenage girls and women victims of domestic violence. *Our mission is to champion these courageous girls and women to lead healthy, successful lives.*

Rocklin, California
800.606.4227 | programs@leaptoexcellence.com
www.leaptoexcellence.com | www.starpartner.org
Sponsor: Leadership Education Action Programs–LEAP
www.LeaptoExcellence.com

Patti Lustig | The Lustig Group: Producing Business Breakthroughs Now | p.52

We coach people and organizations to move beyond their constraints while increasing their productivity, profitability and the difference they make in the world. We deliver a variety of consulting and training programs including the Business Breakthrough Program and Mission Control™ productivity workshops.

Chanhassen, Minnesota
651.631.0404
patti@lustiggroup.com | www.lustiggroup.com

Pamela Bush Davis | Advantage Claims Recovery Group, Inc. | p.54

ACRG is the undisputed industry leader in the recovery of inaccurately denied and incorrectly reimbursed Worker's Compensation claims.

4300 Beltway Drive, Addison, Texas 75001
800.423.2419 | pam@acrginc.com
www.acrginc.com | www.pambushdavis.com

Rosemary McDowell | Contract & Proposal Management Solutions | p.56

C&PMS is a strategic contract, business, and proposal management consulting practice supporting clients in the planning and marketing of programs and solutions. Ms. McDowell has over 30 years experience developing requests for proposals and contracts, preparing responses and pricing, and negotiating and managing contracts with an 85% proposal and a 100% protest win rate over the past 10 years. She contributed to winning proposal efforts with a combined value in excess of $10 billion from FY 2005–FY 2010.

Fairfax, Virginia
703.691.2392 | 571.214.1282
rmcdowell@c-pms.com | www.c-pms.com

Adrienne McGill | Adrienne Clarisse Intimate Boutique | p.58

Passionate about helping women feel good about themselves, we offer a unique and enjoyable shopping experience for fine lingerie and high-end intimate accessories. Whether you come in for an expert bra fitting or looking to spice up your love life, you will enjoy personal attention by our friendly and knowledgeable staff.

531 N. Milwaukee Avenue, Libertyville, Illinois 60048
847.573.8905
adrienne@adrienneclarisse.com | www.adrienneclarisse.com

Joyce C. Mills, Ph.D. LLC | Creative Visionary | p.60

Award-winning therapist, author, speaker, and consultant, Dr. Joyce C. Mills is internationally known for her heart-centered and creative approaches that effect personal and professional transformational change. Her proprietary coaching methods for entrepreneurs, businesses, and organizations are highlighted in her books and products: Reconnecting to the Magic of Life, Butterfly Wisdom®, and her Creative Leaps program.

Scottsdale, Arizona
602.923.2704 | 602.999.8773
drjoyce@drjoycemills.com | www.drjoycemills.com

Lori Palm | Palm Productions, LLC | p.63

Lori Palm is President and owner of Palm Productions, LLC, a professional services firm that focuses on communication, branding, and developing people and business for the 21st century. She created the unique Core Passion® Assessment, a validated, online self-assessment that helps people recognize their real gifts and passion.

6033 Sumter Place, New Hope, Minnesota 55428
612.388.9220
lori@corepassion.com | www.corepassion.com

Michelle Peavy | p.65

Michelle Peavy is a corporate recruiting professional who has expanded her brand to offer keynote speaking where she speaks to your soul through song. She is THE FINAL NOTE.

281.293.0031 | michelle@rimipv.com
www.thefinalnote.biz
www.rimipv.com | www.michellepeavy.com

Mary Pike | Isagenix International | p.66

As a health coach I teach people how cleansing their cells releases harmful impurities, which provides fast, safe weight loss, should that be a goal. The result for everyone, especially thin people, is improved health and well being. The perfect nutrition program for toddlers to seniors.

5114 La Vista , Granbury, Texas 76049
817.559.1404
mary@callmefit.com | www.callmefit.com

Paoola Sefair | Paoo Jewelry | p.68

Paoo is a unique jewelry design company founded by women for women, launched in 2008. Our vision and belief is that through jewelry we have the power to express our personality, feel beautiful, and celebrate and acknowledge our shining moments. We are inspired by bold and courageous women who are making a difference everyday! We draw from their strength and fortitude to design art pieces that capture a sense of joy, fearlessness and confidence.

415.606.4878
psefair@paoo.biz | www.paoo.biz

Sandy Shepard, Esq. | Good Solutions, Inc. and Double Oh! Productions | p.70

I protect your ass-ets with my law firm (GoodSolutions.com), I help you unleash your inner Bond Girl in my lifestyle training practice (BeABondGirl.com), and I turn your Good Intentions into Mail through SendOutCards! (YourCardShark.com)

1537 4th Street, Suite 9, San Rafael, California 94901
415.937.1063 | sandy@goodsolutions.com
www.GoodSolutions.com | www.BeABondGirl.com
www.YourCardShark.com

Gail Speckmann | Full Spectrum Artistry | p.73

"Full Spectrum Artistry" encompasses Gail's artistic offerings. Gail is a national award-winning and internationally- published watercolor artist, instructor, fine art judge, poet, and author of instructional book Wet-into-Wet Watercolor. Also author of HAVE HOPE! Sharing the Journey from Suicidal Depression to a Healed Life, scheduled for release in late 2010.

763.449.8640
info@gailspeckmann.com | www.gailspeckmann.com

Patti Waterbury | Creative Growth Strategies, Inc. | p.74

Creative Growth Strategies, Inc. teaches Christian business owners to be influential leaders that advance the kingdom of God through their business. We help leaders solve problems, make sound organizational decisions and develop strategies so they can live the life they desire, build relationships that expand their sphere of influence, and increase business profitability.

214.289.0125 | pwaterbury@cgstrat.com
www.pattiwaterbury.com | www.themastersnet.com

Jacqueline Wales | The Fearless Factor | p.76

The Fearless Factor is a motivational company for people who are ready to turn off the fear, self-doubt and anxiety and turn on the confidence so you can live your best life now. These unique programs have helped women around the globe develop strong personal success, confident communication and clear visions of their goals.

212.740.7085
Jacqueline@thefearlessfactor.com | www.thefearlessfactor.com

Jenny Fisher Telwar | America's National Teenager Scholarship Organization | p.78

A premier scholarship coach, Telwar is CEO/Owner of America's National Teenager Scholarship Organization. ANTSO awards over $5 million in scholarships annually to deserving young women, ages 9 to 25, in all 53 states and territories. In 2011, she will be expanding to include opportunities for women internationally.

808 Deer Crossing, Nashville, Tennessee 37220
615.405.5107 | 615.370.4338
jennytelwar@me.com | www.nationalteen.com

Karna Sundby | Inner Access | p.80

Karna Sundby is a Personal Life Coach who uses a variety of tools including NLP (Neuro Linguistic Programming) and TPM (Thought Pattern Management), combined with a deeply intuitive approach to help people overcome the obstacles preventing them from living their dreams. Specializing in the areas of Health, Relationships and Creating Abundance, she has worked with clients around the world in person, on the phone and in workshops.

Seattle, Washington
206.915.8531
karna@inneraccess.org | www.inneraccess.org

Karie Wood | Lifekare | p.82

I help people live stronger, healthier lives by connecting them with The Wellness Company, Melaleuca. Better products, safer, less cost–save 30-40% and have them delivered to your door. I have asthma and fibromyalgia, getting chemicals out of my home has improved the quality of my life. The vitamins and supplements have given me a new life, filled with energy.

404 Brookdale Court, The Villages, Florida 32162-1206
651.307.1035 | Karie@lifekare.com

Terri Starnes-Bryant | Microtronic US, LLC | p.85

Microtronic is "Smart Chip/Pre-paid" Technology mainly in regards to Cashless Vending, but also integration with Access Control, POS, Copier, Laundry, Time/Attendance as well as many other applications. My main role is Technical Support and Customer Service.

265 Eastchester Drive, #214, High Point, North Carolina 27262
800.879.3586 | 336.382.1035
terri@MicrotronicUS.com | www.MicrotronicUS.com

Susan K. Younger | Massage Therapist | p.86

Specializing in Structural Integration and Myofascial Release Therapy to reduce pain and achieve muscular balance allowing a higher level of physical integration and mobility.

Design Consultant – quality, efficient and accurate space planning, design and contract construction documents.

1308 Village Creek Dr, Ste 2000, Plano, Texas 75093
214.275.0884
sky@skyounger.com | www.SKYounger.com

Sheri Taber, CEO | The Peak Performance Group, Inc. | p.88

The Peak Performance Group is an award-winning global performance management and executive development firm specializing in strategy development and execution, as well as human and organizational performance excellence.

POB 130806, Tampa, Florida 33681-0806
813.832.2949 | 888.654.3009
Sheri@ThePPGinc.com | www.ThePPGinc.com

Ruth Thoes Vivrett | Walker & Associates | p.90

A financial advisory practice of Ameriprise Financial Services, Inc. Ameriprise offers an ongoing and personalized approach to financial planning that's custom-tailored to each individual client's life and dreams. As an Ameriprise advisor, I help you define your dreams, craft a realistic financial plan to achieve it, and coach you to stay on track toward your goal, whether it's a new home, college for the kids, retirement or something equally important.

1308 Village Creek Dr, Ste 2000, Plano, Texas 75093
469.865.1024
ruth.t.vivrett@ampf.com | www.ameripriseadvisors.com/ruth.t.vivrett

OUR FIVE FAVORITE WORDS:
HOW MAY I HELP YOU?

Central to our philosophy of "giving first and sharing always" is our commitment to lifting others as we climb. This means that as we take every step forward, we must also reach back to bring another along the journey with us. As we grow, others will grow too, which will ensure that as seeds are sown, seeds are simultaneously planted. This will ensure a vibrant, healthy, sustaining future.

We are honored and blessed, as a philanthropic organization, to be part of this extraordinary book, Fearless Women, Fearless Wisdom. Each woman who graces this legacy book—from the cover to the pages—is a personal contributor to the eWomenNetwork Foundation. It's with extreme gratitude that we say "Thank you" to these Fearless Women and especially to our cover girl, Pam Davis, and our artistic photographic visionary, Mary Ann Halpin, who through their own generosity and compassion helps us help so many.

Listed on these pages is just a sampling of non-profit organizations who have received cash grants and in-kind services from the eWomenNetwork Foundation, a 501 (c) (3). Each grant that we award is a direct result of thousands of women throughout the U.S. and Canada who support our local chapters and the Managing Directors who lead our fundraising initiatives. There is truly a powerful network of collaboration built on a foundation of "giving" that allows us to benefit so many. As you experience this Fearless Women book, know that you too are a part of the collective consciousness that makes our world a better place.

Non-profits that have received financial grants from the Foundation:

Acres of Hope, Applegate, CA

Alive, St. Louis, MO

Alpha Pregnancy Resource Center & Maternity Home, Minneapolis, MN

Alternatives to Violence, Loveland, CO

Attitudes & Attire, Dallas, TX

Bay Area Breast Cancer Network, San Jose, CA

Blue Sky Bridge, Boulder, CO

Breakthrough Sacramento, Sacramento, CA

Bridges for Women Society, Victoria, British Columbia, Canada

Brisbane Academy Prep, Charlotte, NC

Business Investment Growth, Inc. (BiGAUSTIN), Austin, TX

C.E.O. Women, Oakland, CA

Career Closets, San Mateo, CA

CARTE, Rocklin, CA

Central Florida Women's Resource Center, Inc., Orlando, FL

Chicks In Crisis, Sacramento, CA

Child Home and Community, Buxmont, PA

Cincinnati Works, Cincinnati, OH

Community Solutions, Morgan Hill, CA

Connections to Success, St. Charles, MO

Covenant House Missouri, St. Louis, MO

Dimensions in Discovery, Inc., Tracy, CA

Dinner Program for Homeless Women, Washington, DC

Down Syndrome Information Alliance (DSIA), Folsom, CA

Eastside Baby Corner, Issaquah, WA

Edmonton Dream Center, Edmonton, Alberta, Canada

Ernestine's Women's Shelter, Toronto, ON, Canada

For Kids Foundation, Reno, NV

FORCE, Tampa, FL

Foreverfamily, Atlanta, GA

Friends of Special Children, Reno, NV

Front Range Exceptional Equestrians Therapeutic, Ft. Collins, CO

Gabriel's Angels, Phoenix, AZ

Genesis House, Chicago, IL

Gift of Hope, Plano, TX

Girls for a Change, San Jose, CA

Jeremiah's Promise, Palo Alto, CA

Joshua Resource Center, Maryville, TN

La Mujer Obrera, El Paso, TX

Larimer County Partners, Inc., Ft. Collins, CO

Leadership Pikes Peak (WCLI), Colorado Springs, CO

Legal Advocates for Abused Women (LAAW), St. Louis, MO

Lydia Dody Breast Cancer Foundation, Northern Front Range, CO

Magnificat Center, St. Louis, MO

Miracles Outreach, Tampa, FL

My Sister's House, Sacramento, CA

N'STEP, Calgary, Alberta, Canada

Oasis for Girls, San Francisco, CA

Powerful Voices, Seattle, WA

Powerstories Theatre, Tampa/St. Petersburg, FL

Project Self-Sufficiency, Northern Front Range, CO

ProKids, Cincinnati, OH

Providence House, Cleveland, OH

Sexual Assault Survivors, Inc., Evans, CO

Shakti Rising, San Diego, CA

Shepherds Counseling Services, Seattle, WA

St. Louise House, Austin, TX

Street's Hope, Denver, CO

Tender Loving Care Homes for Children, Cape Coral, FL

The Child Center, Inc., St. Louis, MO

The Children's Resource Foundation, Houston, TX

The Girls Empowerment Network (GENaustin), Austin, TX

Tragedy Assistance Program for Survivors (TAPS), Tyson's Corner, VA

United Family Services, Lake Norman, NC

Unlimited Potential, Scottsdale, AZ

VinCare Services of Austin Foundation, Austin, TX

WAGES, San Francisco, CA

Wear 2 Start, Victoria, BC, Canada

Well Within, St. Paul, MN

Wheels of Success, Inc., Tampa, FL

Wigs for Kids, Rocky River, OH

Women Helping Women, Houston, TX

Women in Action, San Jose, CA

Women Partnering, Colorado Springs, CO

Women's Empowerment, Sacramento, CA

Women's Resource Agency, Inc., Colorado Springs, CO

WOMEN'S WAY, Philadelphia, PA

Work Options for Women, Denver, CO

WrightChoice Intern Programs, Inc., Columbus, OH

Youth Leadership Foundation, Tyson's Corner, VA

The eWomenNetwork Foundation, a 501(c)(3) organization, is dedicated to supporting the financial and emotional health of women and children in need. Headquartered in Dallas, Texas, the Foundation provides scholarships for "Emerging Leaders" aged 22 – 29 as well as a host of other awards which recognize outstanding achievement and success through its International Femtor Awards program.

www.eWomenNetworkFoundation.org

"I embrace my sword of courage, and move beyond my fear...to help myself...to help the whole world."

Mary Ann Halpin

And the fearless journey continues…